DATE DUE

DEMCO, INC. 38-2931

"*Selling for the Long Run* stands head and shoulders above the run-of-the-mill sales books. This is a blueprint for salespeople who sell complex solutions in a B2B world and want sustained sales success. The book uniquely builds a selling framework that appropriately recognizes the customer's role in the buying-selling relationship and guides the reader through well-crafted strategies to leverage that involvement. If you're in the business of selling complex products or solutions, *Selling for the Long Run* is a blueprint for business success. Don't just read this book—use its principles and strategies every day, and it will fundamentally improve the results you achieve."

—Donal Daly, CEO, The TAS Group

"This book provides a fresh, unique, and contemporary perspective on a previously well-documented subject of selling in a complex business-to-business world. Wendy Reed gives the reader a contemporary road map for the modern-day, buyer-centric sales philosophy. Read it and learn an approach that most certainly enables sales success."

—Richard E. Eldh, Co-President,
SiriusDecisions, Inc.

"The fact that buying behavior has changed dramatically is clear to all sales professionals; how to change the way you sell in response is not. *Selling for the Long Run* offers new insights into how to develop and enrich relationships with clients to not only close more business this year but become the partner of choice going forward as well."

—Jim Dickie, Managing Partner, CSO Insights

"Most sellers know the importance of being aligned with the customer during the buying process, but very few of them have a proven, repeatable strategy for achieving such alignment. In this book, Wendy Reed provides that repeatable strategy and supports it with a set of practical tools that can be used to not only align with the customer but also move to the next level of active collaboration. The level of collaboration outlined in the book goes well beyond what many would consider the traditional concept of buyer-focused selling to a place where the customer is so invested in the process that he or she is an active participant in plotting out the landscape within his or her organization to ensure the business case is established, the resources are put in place, and stakeholder alignment is achieved. The great strength of *Selling for the Long Run* is that it provides an easy-to-follow road map to the kind of customer collaboration that can dramatically change the relationship between buyer and seller and lead to deeper, more successful, and enduring partnerships."

—JOHN GOLDEN, CEO, HUTHWAITE

"Wendy Reed eloquently captures the DNA of sales best practices to the extent that I feel as if she is channeling my own twenty-five years of lessons learned. By addressing the all-important human elements of communication and collaboration, she launches the reader far beyond the traditional seller's role toward a measurable, customer-first business-development mentality that ensures better long-term results. Until more universities offer degree programs in sales effectiveness, this book is required reading for anyone carrying a quota."

—PETER OSTROW, RESEARCH DIRECTOR,
ABERDEENGROUP, A HARTE-HANKS CO.

"Wendy Reed has written a book that captures the maturation of selling technology solutions. As buyers have become more knowledgeable of their needs and available offerings, and more sophisticated in their selection process, technology salespeople haven't kept pace. *Selling for the Long Run* is both a clear reference and a great tool for implementing a collaborative sales approach that aligns with the buyer's view of the world."

—DAVE GOULD, PARTNER, TECH OPERATORS;
FORMER CHAIRMAN AND CEO, WITNESS SYSTEMS

"*Selling for the Long Run* is a sales professional's playbook for success! It presents a rock-solid approach to building and maintaining customer relationships—often reminding you of all the things you know about selling but have forgotten or have been too busy to practice. While other sales books have explored this topic—*Selling for the Long Run* raises the bar as it redefines the rules for customer collaboration, applies new heights of discipline to your sales process, and arms you with the tools necessary to drive long-term success in your customer relationships."

—THOMAS E. NOONAN, PRESIDENT AND CEO,
JOULEX INC.; PARTNER, TECH OPERATORS;
FORMER CHAIRMAN, PRESIDENT, AND CEO,
INTERNET SECURITY SYSTEMS (ISS)

SELLING
FOR THE
LONG RUN

BUILD LASTING CUSTOMER RELATIONSHIPS FOR BREAKTHROUGH RESULTS

WENDY FOEGEN REED
Founder and CEO, InfoMentis, Inc.

New York   Chicago   San Francisco   Lisbon   London   Madrid   Mexico City
Milan   New Delhi   San Juan   Seoul   Singapore   Sydney   Toronto

The **McGraw·Hill** Companies

1 2 3 4 5 6 7 8 9 10 11 12 13 14 15   QFR/QFR   1 9 8 7 6 5 4 3 2 1 0

ISBN   978-0-07-174855-1
MHID   0-07-174855-5

Library of Congress Cataloging-in-Publication Data

Reed, Wendy Foegen.
      Selling for the long run : build lasting customer relationships for breakthrough
results / by Wendy Foegen Reed.
            p.   cm.
      ISBN 978-0-07-174855-1 (alk. paper)
      1. Relationship marketing.   2. Selling.   3. Sales management.   I. Title.

HF5415.55.R425   2011
658.8′02—dc22   2010025356

CONTENTS

FOREWORD

BY GREG NORMAN

Imagine two golfers, both with handicaps of fifteen. They have the same natural ability and training. Their capacity for growth is the same. They have matching resources. They are indistinguishable in every way, save one: the first golfer wants to make the best of his current game; the second wants a complete overhaul.

The first golfer can lower his handicap without making any major changes to his swing. Focusing on his short game and trouble shots will cost him little time. He will see a quick dip in his handicap if he practices putting and sand play, aspects of golf that most influence scoring.

If he plays at least weekly, he can lower his handicap to nine over the course of a year. Not bad. An impressive single digit would sit next to his name. Yet he would be unable to drop much lower than nine.

The second golfer has a loftier goal. He has to study every aspect of golf. He has to hit thousands of practice balls. He must play at least twice a week. But he will be rewarded with a handicap of five, perhaps even lower.

You might be wondering what golf has to do with a book about sales. Golf is about success; it's about winning—one stroke at a time. As a professional golfer and entrepreneur, I understand what it takes to be successful, so when Wendy Reed asked me to read *Selling for the Long Run*, I was happy to oblige.

When I opened the book, I was instantly hooked. Wendy applies many of the same principles in her book that I have applied in my businesses to create success. Wendy puts words to something too many people—golfers and sales professionals alike—overlook: there is a science to success. Sales professionals, like golfers, can apply this science to achieve long-term predictable results.

Wendy's technique will show you a path to improve your game. Her approach has created measured success with her clients. And it will create measured success with your business as well.

No question about it. Wendy Reed's book is for those who want to be superstars, salespeople who know that "not bad" is a far cry from being perfect.

Which golfer are you?

ACKNOWLEDGMENTS

The writing of this book was an extraordinary journey and a career-defining experience. Thank you to everyone who contributed. Special thanks to:

- Carol Ann Weiss for her depth and dedication to countless brainstorming sessions, research, and rewrites, which are clearly manifested in the pages of this book—contributing valuable experience, insight, and stories.
- Steve Maul for his contributions, which are a daily reflection of his ongoing commitment and focus on the creation of training content for InfoMentis clients. Steve's passion for excellence is clearly echoed in the pages of this book and in our clients as they achieve new heights of success.
- Suzanne Rabauer for her relentless drive and determination to complete and publish this book—contributing countless hours to rewrites, review sessions, and management of what often seemed like a never-ending project.
- All those I came in contact with from the start of my professional career at Accenture, Management Science America (MSA)/Dun and Bradstreet Software (DBS), and Hayes Microcomputer, whether a coworker, manager, executive, or customer, each of you (way too many

to mention—but you know who you are) helped to shape and influence my ideas of buying and selling best practices.

○ Each and every InfoMentis client—your loyalty is our success. We listened and learned from your valuable input, enabling us to develop and build upon sales best practices.

INTRODUCTION

THE TALE OF THE CHAIR AND THE ASS

In the past three days, I have spent more quality time with this chair than with my significant other. In fact, this chair is my ass's new best friend. My ass and this chair are molded together. They are one.

But seriously: What is this chair made of? Could it be any more uncomfortable? And why are all the magazines on the coffee table from six months ago?

My cell phone rings, and I almost fall out of my ass's new best friend with excitement.

It's the office.

"Nothing new on this end," I report. "I am still sitting outside of the CIO's office waiting for his signature. I feel pretty sure that he will have this thing done any time now."

"Yes, I know that today is New Year's Eve and that I have only a few hours left to meet the annual quota."

"Yes, I know you have an unruly, cranky gang of anxious people waiting on this contract and just wanting to go home and enjoy a celebration."

"Trust me, this is not where I was planning on spending New Year's Eve."

I feel like I have been wearing these clothes for weeks. Thank God for Wal-Mart and fresh undergarments! When I left for this trip, I expected to be here a day. Fast-forward three days, and here I am: still sitting in this chair, still reading the same outdated magazines, and still hoping we meet our yearly goals.

Meanwhile, on the other side of the wall . . .

Damned salespeople! I cannot believe that woman is still sitting out there. We have told her over and over that this project is important to us, and we have told her that we prefer her solution. She was nothing but accommodating while she was making the sale, but now she wants me to do this on her timeline!

Come to think of it, the more she nags me about this, the less I like her. Maybe we are making a mistake. Will this be the kind of relationship we have—browbeaten into what is best for her? We have been down that path before, and I am not going to let that happen again.

On the other hand, it is the end of the year, and I have her right where I want her. I could certainly negotiate for a lower price. Or I could toy with her: make her think we will do the deal tonight, then worry about the headache and logistics next week. Hell, it is New Year's Eve. I am not going to be held hostage by some sales rep.

I'm going home!

If you have ever worked in a business-to-business sales position, this story brings a familiar vision to your mind. My friends and colleagues who are sales veterans love to exchange sales tales over a beer, and we have heard many a similar tale over and over. Like any veteran in the sales industry, I can relate to any painful story of a buyer dangling a carrot in front of a sales rep.

Those who have not had the pleasure of experiencing a sales career roll their eyes when they hear sales professionals tell their tales.

"It can't be *that* bad," they say. "You guys are exaggerating."

But you know better. It *can* be that bad. At some point or another, we have all been that ass sitting in the chair.

Why Is Selling So Hard?

Looking at the pure fundamentals, acquiring a customer just doesn't seem like it should be that difficult. You have something to offer to a buyer that is cool, different, and valuable. Your marketing team, product development folks, and executives have educated you about the many compelling reasons buyers can no longer live unless they have your solution.

Why is this so hard?

Customer relationships and customer loyalty seem to be topics that generate a great deal of discussion, worry, concern, and debate on both sides of the relationship. Are they elusive? Have the requirements changed, or have the conditions by which the relationship is earned changed?

In the 1980s, you were taught to live by the following mantra: people buy from people they like.

While this might seem obvious, a good litmus test of its validity begins with the answer to the question "Do people buy from people they don't like?"

In 2009, the answer to that was a resounding *yes*.

Jim Hall, a year-after-year overperforming sales representative, came to us at InfoMentis concerned because his competitor was winning far too many deals. In fact, the competitor's representative was stealing some of Jim's longtime clients. According to Jim, the competitor's saleswoman was one of the most obnoxious people that Jim had met. We suspected that Jim might be biased, so we set about to confirm Jim's perception of his competitor. Indeed, several of his past clients—now his competitor's clients—said that Jim's competitor was loud and exceptionally aggressive; they all described her as an old-fashioned mudslinger with little integrity.

Contrast this with Jim. All thought that Jim was nice, polite, well-paced, informed, fun, fair, and respectful.

Neither Jim nor his team members could fathom why buyers would prefer to do business with Jim's competitor. Wouldn't they prefer to buy from someone they like?

We performed a thorough win/loss analysis on the deals that had been lost to this loud, obnoxious, and aggressive saleswoman. We wanted to gain a better understanding of how this could happen. Each buyer reported that although Jim's competitor was aggressive, she was also extremely skilled at understanding her buyers' business needs. She crafted solutions that not only satisfied those needs but exceeded expectations.

Despite misgivings about the obnoxious saleswoman, the buyers were able to overlook all of her objectionable traits and buy what they perceived to be the best solution, even though many of them were Jim's past customers. While his competitor relied on crafting a true solution, Jim relied on his existing relationships and his likeability, so much so that he failed to execute his strategy with 100 percent effort. Did he ignore the customers' business requirements? Not necessarily, but Jim wrongly assumed the buyer would prefer his solution simply because he and the buyer shared a strong positive relationship.

"People buy from people they like," said Jim, defending his position.

We explained to Jim that the old mantra is incomplete, thanks to the power of the Internet and the evolution of the informed buyer.

Buyers used to be educated on new solutions by salespeople, at trade shows, or through magazine articles. Now, with computers commonplace and information readily available, buyers are well educated on new solutions before they ever engage in a conversation with a salesperson. Therefore, the evolution of the buyer has been:

○ People buy from people they like. (Then buyers figured out through bad experiences that they needed to change this approach.)
○ People buy from people they like and trust. (This helped avoid a bad decision but didn't always provide the best solution.)
○ People buy from people who have the best solution even if they don't like them. (However, buyers discovered that some companies don't always stand behind the products, and they experienced great difficulty when left to implement solutions without assistance.)

New World of Selling

In 2010, the mantra has evolved: *buyers buy from salespeople who are likeable, trustworthy, and willing to take care of the buyer's needs, with the latter trumping all.* A buyer might like and trust you, but if the solution is not going to meet his needs, he will prefer to buy from a distasteful individual who is lacking integrity but whose solution does meet his needs.

With this in mind, the strategy becomes obvious: create a situation in which the buyer likes you, trusts you, and feels taken care of. But, given that buyers are traditionally skeptics, how do we do this? Generally, the first contact that a buyer has with you will occur during the sales presentation, when the buyer's defenses are high. Whether you are a seller of consumer goods, business solutions, expensive products, volume products, technology, or services, the sales experience sets the stage for your customer relationships.

In this book, we will examine how you can positively impact your buyers' perceptions of you and your sales organization. Perhaps more importantly, we will look at how to develop world-class customer relationships. Because many organizations receive as much as 80 percent of their revenue from their existing customer base and only 20 percent from new-name accounts, sellers must understand how to make the process a whole lot easier by creating a favorable buying experience. In other words, when you have confident, successful, and happy customers, you are likely to be consulted on the next purchase instead of having to compete for the business.

We will also examine ways that you can bring calm to the chaos of buyer interaction. Most organizations express a desire to have good buyer relationships, but they have either failed to invest enough in the process to build the relationships or do not understand how to structure the process in such a way that it generates the desired outcome. In this book, we will not only explore what activities and processes

make for good buyer relationships, but we will also introduce practical ways to take the actions that make relationships strong. We will look at improving positive exchange
and predictability during the sales cycle as well as examine
how different members of your team can impact buyer perception and improve loyalty.

To my InfoMentis Family—the writing of this book would not have been possible without your never-ending support, creativity, patience, and dedication.

To my husband, Mark, and children, Colin, Kevin, and Grace—in more ways than you can imagine, you have been the inspiration behind the business. Your curiosity and willingness to share have provided me with insight I may not have had alone. I would be remiss, however, if I failed to offer a special dedication to my son Colin, who at the age of seven allowed me to use his computer to start InfoMentis because I did not have one! Your patience in waiting for "your turn" on the computer has clearly paid off.

PART 1

THE PROBLEM OF SILVER BULLET SYNDROME

According to folklore, a silver bullet is the only weapon that can kill vampires, werewolves, and other mystical creatures. As such, the term *silver bullet* has become a metaphor for any surefire antidote to a problem.

The irony, however, is that silver is lighter, harder, and more expensive than lead. In other words, it makes for inferior bullets. The perception is that the silver bullet is the mother of all bullets, when in fact, relying on the silver bullet is like using ten thousand spoons when all you need is a knife.

IN SEARCH OF THE SILVER BULLET

For business professionals interested in maximizing time and resources, looking for the silver bullet—the quickest and easiest way to success—is only natural. But in the words of my first-grade teacher, Mrs. Sykes, "The hurrieder I go, the behinder I get."

Today's businesses are faced with more scrutiny and pressure than ever before. They have to ensure that they are in compliance with the regulatory requirements of the Sarbanes-Oxley Act and the U.S. Securities and Exchange Commission. Their shareholders and the financial community demand financial performance, innovation, and penetration of new markets while, at the same time, these businesses battle the reputation of corporate greed, teetering between shareholder demands and social responsibility.

Aggravating matters, an alarming number of sales professionals are falling below quota performance, as reported by SiriusDecisions, a sales and marketing analysis research firm. This backslide is not surprising. After all, consider these realities of the current business climate:

1. The Internet allows buyers to more easily educate themselves. As a result, they are more knowledgeable and demanding than ever, so they force sales professionals to be more thorough and to provide more proof of their claims.
2. Most organizations aim for maximum coverage with the fewest number of people. The sales process can be expensive. Though the sales process is a company's primary source of revenue, companies often scrutinize costs associated with sales and cut corners in an attempt to hurry the process along.
3. Sales professionals often make pipeline and forecast commitments based upon their own optimistic opinion instead of listening to the buyer.

With such pressure to perform, sales professionals are understandably in constant search of the silver bullet. They think:

○ *If they meet with my executive, I will easily seal the deal.*
○ *Our latest solution will wow them!*
○ *Wait until they see the volume discounts I can offer! This one is in the bag.*

In other words, they are asking themselves: *What's the quickest way to deliver this solution? What is the silver bullet I can use to win this deal?*

If the truth be told, most sales professionals are always on the lookout for silver bullets, assuming that if they can control the situation through a quick and easy hook, they can skip steps, reduce the amount of work, reduce the cost, and win contracts.

Silver bullets may indeed solve a particular dilemma at a particular time, but the search for the mysterious silver bullet ultimately leads to a shortcut culture fraught with uncalculated risks that turn the shortcut into the long way around. The time, money, and resources spent on shortcuts are incalculable, as most organizations merely chalk up these expenditures to the cost of doing business before moving on to more shortcuts and silver bullets.

And most importantly, the premise behind the silver bullet—that the sales professional can control the sales cycle—leads to an artificial feeling of security. Silver bullet syndrome tricks the seller into believing that a brilliant presentation, an unbelievable success story, or a cool product feature will seduce the buyer into quickly closing the deal.

A leading solution provider I'll call Solution Brokers was one shot away from winning a bid with a major telecommunications buyer, which I'll call Hargrove, who was looking for a software solution for its customer-support needs. In preparation for the final meeting that would determine whether Solution Brokers or its competitor would win the contract, Hargrove's vice president of information technologies, Anna, sent Solution Brokers a list of seven points. Solution Brokers spent a few hours preparing a stellar presentation that would address each of these seven points.

We definitely have this in the bag, thought the lead sales representative, John, prior to the meeting.

When members of Solution Brokers' sales team arrived, they noticed that the buyer's team consisted of twice as many people as expected. Half of Anna's committee were new faces Solution Brokers had never seen.

John kicked off the presentation, beginning with the first of seven points. Four hands immediately shot into the air. The new faces had all sorts of questions about the background information that Solution Brokers had provided in previous meetings.

John briefly and politely answered each question before quickly moving on to the next. More hands, more questions, more answers. John tried to remain in control of the process, growing frustrated with his inability to steer the buying team back on track. Eventually, he became defensive, hoping that Anna—who had submitted the seven points—would step in and steer the meeting in the right direction. Unfortunately, Anna remained silent, allowing the new people on Hargrove's committee to consume all of the limited time.

We'll never get through the seven points at this rate, John thought.

And he didn't. The meeting ended with frustration. Because John had given only brief answers to the impromptu questions, Hargrove's new team members felt that their concerns were not given proper consideration; likewise, the sellers were irritated that their presentation was thrown to the wayside.

In the end, Solution Brokers' largest competitor, which I'll call Outstanding Options, won Hargrove's business, and Solution Brokers' third-quarter sales slipped far behind projections.

Solution Brokers made a crucial mistake, one that they share with many sales professionals, and one that is rooted in the belief that the seller can control the process. Early in the relationship-building process, sales professionals often make this critical mistake that, if avoided, would drastically change the course of the sales experience and the ongoing relationship with the customer.

That frequent mistake?

Too often, sellers neglect the buyers' perspective by trying to control the process instead of responding to the buyers' requirements. Though seductive, the silver bullet presented by the seller causes many buyers to miss the value of the solution because they have no time to internalize the offerings. Instead of aligning a solution with a buyer's need, sellers simply focus on the silver bullet, scratching their heads when it fails.

In a similar example, Hargrove, which also needed a software solution to address its contact management needs, was in the middle of a meeting with a large enterprise software company we'll call Maltern Software, whose contact management software had been deployed successfully years earlier.

Because Maltern was excited about the next generation of its software, which would be released in one year, it spent the meeting showcasing the bells and whistles that would be released in the next generation. Maltern completely overlooked the features and benefits of its existing software, which could be deployed immediately.

If we can get Hargrove excited about the new release, they won't be able to turn us down, thought Maltern's sales representatives.

Unfortunately, because Hargrove interpreted the focus on the upcoming release to mean that Maltern Software did not have an *existing* solution that would work, Hargrove chose another vendor that had an inferior solution but a solution that was obviously available immediately.

Symptoms of Silver Bullet Syndrome

Silver bullet syndrome can grow at either a corporate or an individual level. In either case, it is often hard to recognize because self-diagnosis is clouded by rationalization and bias. How can you tell if you have or are promoting silver bullet syndrome? There are telltale signs.

You are a victim of silver bullet syndrome if:

- **You start each sales encounter with your standard solution pitch.** Victims of silver bullet syndrome ignore the fact that each client is unique. Instead, they consider their solution better, faster, stronger, and sexier, not paying attention to how and whether it aligns with the buyer's needs.
- **You start each sales encounter with your company's story.** Victims of silver bullet syndrome ignore the fact that the buyer likely has already done due diligence about your company. Instead, they spend valuable time bragging about their company's accomplishments, which are old news, boring, and irrelevant.
- **You use lots of sales support resources, but you have little sales results.** Experience shows that sales professionals who rely the most on support resources (people other than the salesperson who help sell the deal) are the least productive. These professionals are likely relying

on shortcuts, hoping that the sales support team will sell the product or service on their behalf. The most productive sales professionals use the least resources because they spend time up front learning about the product, region, or service; setting and managing expectations; and qualifying the buyer. In short, they work harder than those who lean heavily and often on sales support resources.

Activity

List your top three sales professionals, as well as those who are the least productive. Then ask your sales support resource team to list the top users of sales support, as well as those who use the least. Chances are, you will notice a direct inverse correlation between use of sales support and productivity. The reason for this inverse relationship? Your bottom producers are victims of silver bullet syndrome, relying on the sales support team to do their jobs for them.

• **You are in urgent mode, especially at month's or quarter's end.** Sales professionals who dedicate all their resources to month- or quarter-end closing are in urgent mode, likely taking shortcuts and applying significant resources to meeting their quotas rather than following a well-defined process, expending a great deal of effort at a time when it makes the least impact. Shifting the effort to the front end of the sales impact allows sales professionals to enjoy a greater impact.

• **You meet every buyer request with no trade in exchange for your services.** Our clients are surprised to learn that the over-serve mentality is a silver bullet. Too often, sales professionals simply assume that if they give their buyers the world, the buyers will jump at the chance to give their business to the seller. The truth of the matter is this: the buying and selling process should not be mutually exclusive, and a seller should not give a buyer anything without asking for something in return. Asking for something in return provides a dual purpose: it not only moves the process along, but it also helps eliminate the buyer's expectations of a discount. If a seller gives and gives without asking for anything in return, the seller unintentionally trains the buyer to ask for discounts. If the seller refuses, the buyer becomes outraged because the sales professional has changed the rules in the final lap.

- **You encounter surprises in the sales process.** Victims of silver bullet syndrome rarely realize that their activities do not move them forward in the buying process. Instead, they assume that the buyer is at the same point in the process as the seller. Because this is rarely the case, silver bullet victims first assume that they know their buyers' problems, offering solutions before their buyers ask for them. As the process continues, the sellers begin to feel as if their clients' needs are never clearly communicated and are always changing. Because they do not validate that their activities will advance the buying process, these sales professionals experience surprises, such as forecast slippages.

An organization is working within silver bullet syndrome if:

- The bulk of its time is spent focusing on the end of the sales process, with only minimal time spent up front.
- It notices decreasing deal size.
- It engages in product or service feature wars.
- It invests in many different sales methodologies with limited or undocumented business results.
- It has unpredictable forecasts both in terms of total revenue and revenue per transaction.
- It provides reactive executive involvement.
- It focuses on internally developed value messages that must be delivered to every prospect and customer.

Negative Effects of Silver Bullet Syndrome

Consider the trickle-down effect of a silver bullet.

In this very real example (illustrated in the following figure), imagine that your sales organization finds itself in a *buyers' market*, meaning that buyers have more choices and can select from a larger group of sellers. You, as well as your competitors, are hungry for a sale.

Because the buyer has many choices, you are in a *highly competitive situation*. The buyer has many choices and many solutions that might appear to work. As such, sellers must differentiate themselves from the competition or risk losing.

Because the solutions look the same, and the sales cycle is aggravated by several indications that the competitor may

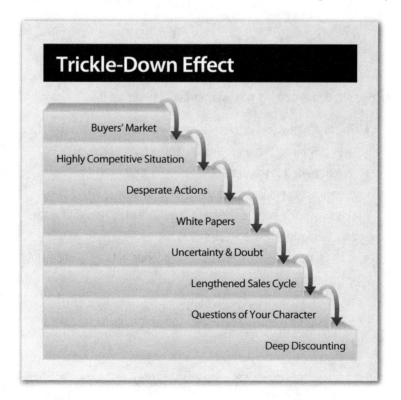

Trickle-Down Effect

- Buyers' Market
- Highly Competitive Situation
- Desperate Actions
- White Papers
- Uncertainty & Doubt
- Lengthened Sales Cycle
- Questions of Your Character
- Deep Discounting

be winning, the pressure to close the sale by quarter end is intense.

In an effort to hurry the process along so that you can quickly win or take the lead, you attempt bold or *desperate actions*, looking for the silver bullet that shoots you ahead of the pack.

When you release a *white paper* comparing your solution to the competition, you are sure that your silver bullet will prove that your solution has true appeal—even though it was delivered in a negative fashion. After all, you are conditioned to believe your solution is the best. This mother-and-apple-pie devotion to your company might earn you points with the top cheese in your organization, but the truth is that your solution differs only slightly from the competitor's.

Many times, a silver bullet is used as a vehicle to instantly turn a negative situation into a positive one. In this situation, the white paper paid little attention to the worst possible outcome, failing to answer the question "Have I earned the right to compare my solution to the competition's in a trusted way versus a negative way?" Instead, the silver bullet was used as a trick to gain a winning spot.

But rather than move the process along, the white paper caused the buyer to panic. The buyer had not considered the elements discussed in your white paper. What else was it missing? Perhaps it needed to start over from scratch.

The white paper succeeded only in transitioning the sales cycle from one of business value to one of *fear, uncertainty,* and *doubt.*

The buyer is forced to reevaluate its considerations.

Now the buyer is irritated. You have created chaos in the sales cycle with the white paper, and when the buyer began comparing the solutions, it realized the two choices were quite similar. And now your company's character is called into question. You have confused the process and *lengthened the sales cycle.*

As well, you have shifted the focus of the buyer away from solution value. The buyer now is forced not only to validate the solution value but also the integrity and *character* of each seller.

In the end, you try to make up for the confusion by *deeply discounting* your solution. Sure, perhaps you engaged in all the recommended activities in the sales cycle. You could even say you went down fighting. Or perhaps you saved the deal with a discount. In the end, though, one way or another your silver bullet lengthened the sales cycle, shortchanged value, and left money on the table—all in an effort to take a shortcut.

In this situation, you overlooked the buying cycle, instead trying to control the process with your sales cycle through a silver bullet (in this case, a white paper). You didn't consider the negative impact when you analyzed it from the buyer's perspective.

CHAPTER 1

The Silver Bullet and the Buyer's Perspective

"I found out that if you are going to win the game, you had better be ready to adapt."

—Scotty Bowman, most winning coach in NHL history

The key to avoiding the silver bullet is to acknowledge that the buyer has the money and the seller does not. Hence, the buyers make decisions about you and your solution, and they are in control of the sales process.

Therefore, no world-class sales process exists, only a world-class buying process. The silver bullet is nothing more than superstition. In fact, the term *sales process* is misleading. The sales team does not drive the process— the buyer does. The key to mastering this process—to taming the tornado that often ensues upon embarking on a new sales process—is to learn how to align your sales process with the buyer's process. This starts by your understanding the buyer's perspective.

Unfortunately, salespeople and teams have a tough reputation to overcome. We often hear the following complaints about sales teams:

○ "The sales team was arrogant. They kept telling us what they wanted to tell us, not what we needed to know."
○ "The sales reps are always talking. They talk nonstop about themselves, their company, and their solutions. They talk, talk, talk, but they never listen, which means they do not understand our business."
○ "Every time we ask them a question, we get a slightly different answer, which makes it hard to know the truth and trust the sales team."

This reputation stems from a central assumption: as sellers, we often assume that because we want to develop strategic relationships with buyers, the buyers want to develop strategic relationships with us. We are so besotted with our awesome solutions and the sexy features that we believe the benefits are intuitively obvious to all of our buyers. As a result, instead of helping our buyers understand how the solution will solve their problem, we jump straight into what vendors think is cool and ignore the buyers' perspective.

We neglect to understand what the buyer perceives or believes to be true.

Critical to the ability to develop a relationship is our ability to put ourselves in the buyers' shoes, culture, and business. In doing so, we can begin to understand the buyers' perspective.

The Two Critical Questions

When sellers identify opportunities, they immediately begin obsessing about budgets and deadlines, busying themselves by worrying about closing sales and moving on to the next big deal. Though the seller might see the obvious connection between her solution and the buyer's challenge, the seller's mentality does little to assuage the buyer's fear that the proposed solution will not address his specific need.

Instead, the salesperson inadvertently sends a loud message to the buyer: *I'm going to love you and leave you by the side of the road.*

The seller can begin to rectify this by asking two critical questions. The first question is directed to the buyer.

"What Happened in Your Business That Triggered Your Need for a Solution?"

This question not only helps the buyer feel understood, but answers to this simple question reveal the buyer's needs and goals.

Surprisingly, most sales professionals cannot name their top three buyers' business goals. Can *you*? If you were given the challenge of listing the business objectives of your top three buyers, would this information be ingrained in your mind, or would you struggle to come up with one of their goals, much less three?

Activity

Put yourself in the shoes of your top three buyers. Now see if you can complete the following statement on their behalf:

The top three indicators of my success as it relates to my business are:

Top Buyer 1   **Top Buyer 2**   **Top Buyer 3**

_____ _____ _____

_____ _____ _____

_____ _____ _____

If you cannot complete this activity, you are likely a victim of silver bullet syndrome, always searching for a quick and easy way to seduce buyers into doing business with you.

Next comes the second critical question, which you—the salesperson—must be able to answer.

"What Do My Prospects, Buyers, and Customers Think About My Solution, My Company, and Me?"

At the end of the day, your own opinion of your solution and company does not matter. Your competitors' and colleagues' opinions do not matter. Your *prospects* are the ones who will decide to spend money with you, or not. Your *buyers* are the people who will share opinions with prospects and create your reputation. Your *customers* are the people who will validate or dispute information about your solution and your customer service skills.

Such opinions are crucially important. Yet an astounding number of sales professionals lack insight into how they are perceived by these most important people.

The Buyer's Perspective of Salespeople

The second critical question requires the salesperson to consider not only the buyers' perception of his personality, competence, reliability, and the like but also the perception of his sophistication as a sales professional.

As sales representatives grow personally and within their organization, they evolve from communicating product solutions to business solutions to strategic solutions to the buyer.

As indicated in the pyramid, the majority of sales professionals are perceived as *product solution* representatives. Most sales professionals start

Categorizing Sales Professionals
The Buyer's View

Strategic
Solution Professional

Business
Solution Professional

Product
Solution Professional

out in this category because they need time to evolve their business knowledge and grow their abilities. Here are some characteristics of product solution professionals:

- They can intelligently discuss and represent the products and services they sell.
- They have some awareness of other customers who have used their products and services.
- They can articulate some basic business and financial benefits and points of impact offered by their product or service.

Product solution representatives are typically good communicators who professionally present and demonstrate their product and services. They have basic organization skills, are decent with follow-up tasks and communication, and bond well with buyers. If they are to do business with solution representatives, buyers expect them to be knowledgeable and professional.

As you can see, the perception of product solution representatives is not negative. The downside is that once a sales professional is pigeonholed as a product solution representative, the professional has a difficult time convincing buyers that he can be more strategic. As well, a product solution representative will not have much success meeting with executives on the buying team. Instead, executives will delegate the meeting to someone lower on the totem pole.

The next category of sales professional—the perceived *business solution* professional—is more valuable to the buyer and is considered a problem solver. A business solution professional is more focused on value for the buyer. The differences in perception of the business solution professional over the product solution representative include the following:

- They have a clear understanding of how buyers and businesses use their solutions.
- They are credible when it comes to business discussions, and they exhibit strong business acumen.
- They can help the buyers craft a business case for their solution.

As far as communication abilities, business solution professionals not only have an awareness of presentation skills and organization, but they also practice these in every exchange and communication with the buyer. They share information and can differentiate their solution; provide alternatives; and listen, align, and personalize business benefits and advantages of their solution. Business solution professionals might have potential access to a buying executive, but they will not be seen as strategic partners. That is, while the buying executive might accept a phone call or meeting from a business solution professional, the executive is not likely to reach out to a business solution professional to solve a problem.

Though being perceived as a business solution professional bodes well, the *strategic solution* sales professional sits at the top of the pyramid because there are fewer of these in the sales industry. The relationships between strategic solution sales professionals and their buyers provide tremendous benefit to both vendor and buyer, but they don't happen overnight, and they are hard to come by. A strategic solution sales professional:

- Understands industry issues and challenges
- Can help individual buyers understand business
- Adds value to the buyer's organization
- Understands and can affect the buyer's political infrastructure
- Will strategize *with* a buyer, not *for* a buyer
- Looks at short-, mid-, and long-term challenges and objectives that impact the buyer
- Demonstrates exceptional communication skills
- Might be promoted to an executive position

Strategic solution sales professionals typically have a more developed ability to listen, internalize, and adjust on the fly. They think in a business sense, not a product or solution sense, and they act in the same manner. As such, a buyer considers the strategic professional to be a trusted advisor.

Without knowing which of these three categories she falls into, the salesperson cannot address any shortcomings the buyer might perceive. However, if a salesperson knows how she is perceived, she can: (1) take measures to change her behavior and move up the pyramid and (2) accurately measure whether her behavior is working.

How can the seller determine into what category the *executive* buyer places her? The following pyramid represents the outcome of meetings with buyers based on the buyers' perception of the sales professional or sales team.

As well as knowing how they are perceived, sellers must also take care to remember that the buyers likely know much less about the solutions than the sellers do. If a seller assumes a buyer knows more than he does, the seller will fail to draw the obvious connection between the need and solution.

In our discussions with sales and marketing teams, we always evaluate the seller's processes for analyzing wins and losses. More often than not, the seller's evaluation methods are confined to a debriefing of the sales team, a skewed source that often ignores the most important part of the equation: the buyer's opinion! If a deal is lost, the salesperson tends to blame it on the product or service; if the deal is won, the salesperson attributes the success to a superior sales strategy and the stellar sales professional leading the team to victory. Regardless of whether these are truths or exaggerations, one thing is certain: the feedback is most often *not* coming from the source—the buyer.

An organization must always ask the buyer for this feedback. For instance, a seller might simply ask the buyer questions like these: "What do you know about our solution?" "What have you heard about our company?"

By engaging the buyer in a dialogue, sales team members gather critical information about how they are being perceived by those in power or those who have a vote.

Before you can make any significant improvements in the way that you interact with prospects and customers, you have to interact with them and listen to what they have to say! In fact, this entire book is dedicated to helping you communicate with and gather feedback from current and potential customers. Remember how you felt your first day on the job? You were likely overwhelmed, confused, and lacking information about where to start. Remember that day, and imagine that your buyers are just as overwhelmed and confused. In this way, you can feed them the critical information they need to do their job and make a decision about your solution.

Let's take a look at two examples that illustrate why this feedback is so important.

Situation #1: A seller (Maltern Software) who provides contact management technology believes it has great solutions—and it does. The company loves to give product demonstrations that highlight all the product's bells and whistles. They believe that their technology really sizzles.

Yet the buyer—Hargrove—perceives "sizzle" a little differently. Read what Anna had to say when we interviewed her on behalf of the technology company:

"We really liked Maltern's sales team. We know the organization is reputable, but the solution's complexity did not address our requirements. We felt as though we had already given the company exactly what we needed in the way of our requirements. But what we heard and saw during the demonstration confused us. We did not need all those features, and the solution seemed too complicated. Most of what they showed us did not apply, so we did not think they listened to our needs."

Of course, "upselling" and expanding the deal are important parts of the selling process, but this is a classic example of a difference in perception. The buyer did not think the bells and whistles sizzled. To the contrary, Hargrove felt that the bells and whistles made the solution convoluted and confusing.

I hear these same sentiments over and over from buyers. The sales team perfects its sale pitch and then acts on autopilot, delivering the same "sizzling" spiel over and over without engaging the buyer and reacting to his signals.

Liken this to your commute to work, which you likely have perfected. You know the quickest route, each street sign, and each traffic light. Have you driven to the office only to arrive and realize you have little memory of the turns you made? The commute is so ingrained in your brain that you take little notice of the scenery. You simply go through the motions.

Yet, when you drive to a new location, you are focused. You pay attention to each street sign. You are altogether aware of the traffic signals. If you make the wrong turn, you quickly take the appropriate steps to get back on track. When you arrive, you can distinctly remember the drive. You are fully engaged.

The first example—the familiar commute—is easier. It is certainly more comfortable. Yet when engaging a buyer, the second is the better analogy: the sales process is *always* a new drive. Yet too many salespeople are on autopilot, delivering the same presentation over and over again. They are so comfortable with their own solution knowledge that they put little attention on engaging themselves in the buyer's needs.

Let's take a look at one more example.

Situation #2: Hargrove recently released an RFP to hire a public relations firm to the tune of $1,250,000. The CEO expected several of the seven public relations firms submitting proposals to focus on Hargrove.

Hargrove's intent was to use the RFP as a filter for the seven companies that looked interesting, but the CEO also wanted to see which of the seven called her to learn more about the business before responding to the RFP. The CEO was surprised when only three of the seven called her to ask questions or uncover more about the business.

To her delight, the three firms that took the initiative to contact her included in the RFP the knowledge they gleaned from that conversation, so Hargrove invited them—and two others—to come back for a second-round interview. Of the seven firms that submitted proposals, two used a boilerplate proposal that did not address the clearly stated objectives of the RFP. Hargrove removed them from consideration.

The CEO invited the five whose proposals showed initiative to spend an hour with her buying team for deeper discovery so that the sellers could prepare their presentations.

When these companies delivered their presentations, the CEO was shocked. Hargrove's budget would have boosted each of these firms' bottom lines. After all, this was no small-potatoes job; Hargrove meant business. Yet four of the five companies delivered standard presentations that could have been delivered to any buyer. The sellers failed to incorporate basic information such as Hargrove's mission. They certainly did not demonstrate an understanding of the roles of the executives, nor did they understand the client base.

The company Hargrove selected was a complete standout. Keep in mind that this company did not have a secret recipe. The actions they took were basic. They simply named Hargrove's clients, clearly understood the company's mission, and delivered specific examples of how their firm would address Hargrove's needs.

All the other public relations firms wasted the CEO's time with discovery and presentations that focused on the seller. One of the sellers was extraordinarily competent and professional. Its team's knowledge of the industry was unsurpassed. Yet they lost the deal.

Why?

The CEO's buying team had the *perception* that this sales team did not listen to them. Had the team simply asked Hargrove about the company's needs and responded accordingly by reiterating this information when presenting the solution, Hargrove would have learned how it could benefit from the seller's solution.

This happens every day to thousands of companies. The sales teams are moments away from connecting with buyers. They have all the ingredients but one. The sales teams are smart, competent, aware, and reliable, but they have different perceptions about what is needed, and missing this one critical ingredient costs them a sale.

Think of it this way: Imagine again that you are driving, this time to the grocery store, a drive you probably take at least weekly. Think about what you see and feel along the way. Now imagine the drive back home. Again, consider the things you see and how you feel. Though you are proceeding down the same road you traveled on your way to the store, you focus on different things; the scenery, views, and emotions related to the route seem different.

On the way to the grocery store, you might pay little attention to your neighborhood. You might feel anxious. *I hope the lines at the store aren't too long. Ugh—I have only two days a week to spend time with my family, and I have to go to the grocery store, of all places. If I'm not in and out, I'm going to be really annoyed. I hate running errands. I wish this car in front of me would just go!*

On the way home, having encountered no long lines, you are likely more relaxed. You might turn on the radio and sing along. As you drive past your neighbor's home, you feel comforted. You notice the children playing in the yard, the new truck in your other neighbor's driveway, the changing colors of the leaves. All of this was present when you drove to the store, but your focus was elsewhere.

The same phenomenon happens to vendors and buyers "proceeding down the same road." Even though the product or solution they want is exactly the same as the one you offer, their perceptions of the scenery are different.

The Eye of the Buyer

The focus of this book is on teaching you to consider the eye of the buyer, recognizing that it is very different from that of the seller. Buyers have their best interests in mind as they move through the evaluation process, and, as you might have guessed, sellers have their best interests in mind when moving through the selling process.

These two interests do not necessarily align with one another. The following table demonstrates how these two interests typically misalign. While buyers are concerned with differentiating among the solutions they will evaluate, sellers are concerned with preparing a great presentation. While buyers are focused on finding solutions that will maximize the investment, add value to the organization, and minimize business disruption, sellers are concerned with closing the deal.

When buyers explain why they did not buy from specific sellers, their explanations almost always fall into one of the following five answers. Consider that each of these scenarios indicates a conflict between the eye of the seller and the eye of the buyer.

1. **The vendor talked about what it wanted to sell, not about what the buyer needed.** The vendor thinks: *This sizzle is so cool. I can't wait to tell the buyer all about it! I hope I don't forget anything!*

BUYER'S FOCUS	SELLER'S FOCUS
"What do we really need to address as our key business requirements?"	"How will I make my quota? Where will I find my leads?"
"How do we determine who has the best solution?"	"Does the buyer have the budget and authority to make any purchases this year?"
"How do we understand the specific differences among the solutions we evaluate?"	"I need to prepare a killer presentation showing all the coolest aspects of my solution."
"How do we understand the risks associated with implementing each of the solutions?"	"I need to make sure they know how much better our solution is than any competitive alternative."
"How do we know whom to trust?"	"I need access to the decision makers and executives."
"How do we determine the resources necessary to implement the solution successfully?"	"I need to close this deal before the end of the quarter."
"How do we measure the project's level of success?"	"I need to pass the deal to customer support and move on to the next deal."

But as we saw earlier, a vendor creates a huge risk when controlling what the buyer sees instead of collaborating to determine the buyer's need. When a seller rigidly follows a sales script, a buyer is forced to consider solutions that do not align with the buyer's process or needs. A buyer cannot possibly absorb dozens of bells and whistles in a new solution. In fact, asking a buyer to incorporate all of the bells and whistles of your product or service might feel overwhelming. The buyer thinks: *What? I don't have time to incorporate all of this into my business. This is just more trouble than it is worth.*

The buyer needs a fast, clear, and simple solution that is easily implemented with benefits that are immediately recognized. The seller must show how the product's features and the buyer's needs are aligned.

2. **The buyers were skeptical that the vendor could deliver what they needed.** Too often, the sales team has dozens of people, yet the buyers are doubtful of their ability to perform. With a team so large, how can that be?

   Executives expect salespeople to marshal the right resources at the right time. The buyers do not expect one person to be the expert on everything, but they do expect their key contact to listen to their needs and assess the resources needed to address their specific needs. If the sales team requires an army to simply listen to the buyers' needs and locate the appropriate resources, the buyers will doubt the account manager's resourcefulness.

3. **The buyers didn't like the sales approach.** Have you ever noticed that most sales processes and methodologies are one of the best-kept secrets from buyers? Buyers have negative perceptions of sales approaches because they perceive that they are about and for the seller. If a seller opens up the sales cycle, creating a collaborative cycle in which both buyer and seller actively participate, the buyer feels ownership for the sales approach.

4. **Key buyers in the decision process had little or no contact with the salesperson.** As part of the due diligence, a seller must learn who the decision makers are. Though interacting with them is undoubtedly more stressful and less comfortable, approaching only the friendly team members is ineffective.

5. **All the vendors looked the same, so the buyers based their decision on price alone.** As Hargrove experienced when trying to hire a public relations firm, few providers rise to the occasion to show their advantages. If the buyers perceive that all solutions are the same, they focus on price alone.

In the chapters that follow, I present a process for overcoming the problems associated with the traditional seller-centric sales cycle. You will learn how to do the following:

o Slow down and move at the buyer's pace instead of yours. After all, the process is not all about you.
o Align your sales process with the buyer's process.
o Understand the buyer's business challenges.
o Connect with the people who vote.
o Assess your competitive landscape.
o Connect the dots by tying actions to strategies.
o Collaborate on the game plan.
o Position your value.
o Measure your advancement with the buyer.

In adopting these tactics, you will learn to win without firing a single silver bullet.

CHAPTER 2

The Gap Between Buyers and Sellers

"It's not where you start—it's where you finish that counts."
—Zig Ziglar, known as "America's Motivator" and
author of twenty-nine books and numerous
audio and video recordings

In business commerce, the process of exchanging money for goods has been around for centuries. However, the dynamics of that exchange have changed dramatically over recent years, in part for the following reasons:

o **Information is more accessible.** In the "old days," the first salesperson to show up had a significant advantage. Today's consumers have access to more information and can easily research alternatives, forcing the process to change.

- ○ **As a result, buyers are more demanding.** They have done this before, have more resources, and are much more sophisticated.
- ○ **Competition is strong.** Advertising and branding are much bolder than ever. Providers proactively discuss the advantages their solutions have over other solutions. They seek to gain an emotional advantage much earlier in the process.

When you look at these new dynamics, your immediate reaction might be that you have to be quicker, more agile, better, and faster than the next guy. While it is true that you certainly must be responsive, do you have to rush?

Roller Coaster or Ferris Wheel?

Growing up, I was fond of roller coasters—they satisfied that need for speed. However, the most memorable rides were the ones I shared with friends chatting away on the Ferris wheel. Time spent on a Ferris wheel most certainly yields more insight than time spent on a roller coaster. For the same reason, more business is conducted on a golf course than on a tennis court. And though the seller might have a need for speed, roller coasters fail to provide the comfort of a more relaxed give-and-take. A Ferris wheel allows the buyer and seller to work slowly but steadily toward mutual goals and a mutual deadline.

Velcro Is Better than Teflon

When it comes to gaining trust and confidence, a seller must provide enough substantive information that the buyers understand how and why they should engage with the seller. If you simply throw a ton of data and information at the buyers, failing to take the time to filter what is really relevant and important to the buyers, your information will simply slide right past the buyers like Teflon.

But if you slow down and collaborate so that each of you is participating in a mutually beneficial, cooperative agreement, you create "stickiness," allowing the buyers to internalize the suggestions that you share with them.

As soon as our sales clients start to rattle off the dozens of reasons their product or service is so wonderful, we quickly stop them and tell them to ask these two following questions from the buyers' perspective:

○ "So what?"
○ "Who cares?"

Their initial response is usually the same: "They want to be successful, and we have the strongest track record. We bring experience to the table."

They talk, and talk, and talk, rushing to show their solution's superiority, never slowing down to explain why the solution is significant from the buyers' perspective.

Imagine that you are at a trade show featuring the latest models of luxury cars. As you walk from booth to booth, the car salespeople try to steal a minute or two of your time, throwing information your way about the features and functions of their cars. They talk. You listen.

The first salesman focuses on the leather seats and six cup holders his model provides. Then he gives you a Tactical Benefit of the car: you and your entire family can comfortably eat hamburgers without having to hold a drink between your legs!

> **Tactical Pain** = The tasks, situations, or processes that prevent a buyer from achieving key business requirements.
>
> **Tactical Benefits** = The solution to the Tactical Pain.

What the salesman fails to recognize is that you do not eat in your car because you like to limit the amount of time and money you spend at the car wash. Unfortunately, he assumed this benefit solved a one-size-fits-all Tactical Pain. But the pain did not apply to you, nor do the features that the other salespersons pitch to you.

Because they are not taking time to solicit information from you, their solutions don't stick. They are Teflon, and you spend your time thinking: *So what? Who cares?*

Let's take a look at how another salesperson turns Teflon into Velcro.

The next saleswoman recognizes that she has only a limited amount of time with you. Rather than wasting it on a Tactical Benefit that may or may not be relevant, she asks you questions about your lifestyle. You tell her that you spend a lot of time in your car with clients, which means appearance is important to you. As well, your job is high stress. Between your family and your career, you have little personal time. When alone in the car, you like to listen to audiobooks as well as your favorite tunes on your iPod.

This saleswoman now has a perfect opportunity to explain how her solution and your unique needs are like two sides of Velcro: when pressed together, they become one complete solution. She explains that the car features ten speakers, which means you can have different levels of volume depending on who is in the car and where they are seated. As well, the car comes with four complimentary coupons for free detailing. Quarterly, the car dealership will pick the car up from your home or office, clean and detail the car, and return it to your office two hours later.

Voilà! She has offered a Tactical Benefit that fits your needs. Your life is often hindered by all the small tasks you must complete regularly, including the mandatory car wash necessary to keep your car impressive-looking for clients. This Tactical Pain seems relieved (at least in part) when you consider the free and convenient quarterly detailing.

To have Velcro, you must communicate the solutions that are relevant to the pain that the product or service relieves, as well as the subsequent benefits of the solution. If a salesperson had simply talked without slowing down to ask you a few questions, his or her solution would not have stuck.

Why Going Slowly Is Really Fast

From these examples, perhaps you can already see why slowing down allows a person to accomplish more in a shorter amount of time. Going slowly yields several possible outcomes:

○ Because you spend the time on the front end, it's much shorter on the back end, which makes the overall process shorter.

- The size of the opportunity or engagement often gets larger. If your business sells both a solution and support for that solution, often the sales representative lowballs the cost of maintenance and support. In a rush to sign a contract, they provide discounts on services and do not have the time to assess the proper price, much less communicate the service provisions to the buyer. By going slowly, the sales representative can defend his position, remind the client of the value of the service, and increase the opportunity.

- You set a precedent and elevate the buyer's expectations of its vendors, which in and of itself is a competitive advantage. When Hargrove requested proposals for a public relations firm, only three of the seven recipients called Hargrove's CEO to ask questions. And only one used the information in its proposal and presentation. The vendor spent more time with the CEO on the front end, which meant the vendor spent more time preparing the proposal. The CEO felt a personal connection to the vendor. When other potential vendors failed to spend the same time with the CEO, the entire buying team felt disconnected from them.

- You understand your buyer's needs faster, allowing you to provide solutions with a higher business value than other providers.

- Because you have documented the business situation, the buyers' needs, and the challenges they will have with your sales cycle, you can position yourself to demonstrate how your services align with their unique needs.

Very simply, both you and your buyer can hit the ground running.

Let's talk about each of these benefits by taking a look at Outstanding Options and its relationship with Hargrove.

Larry was hired as a senior account manager for Outstanding Options, a company that sells a variety of software solutions. As Larry began reviewing his client files, he became less and less pleased with his company's record with Hargrove.

The track record was less than stellar, and when Larry called to introduce himself to Anna, he learned that she felt oversold and not understood.

"In the past, Outstanding Options rushed through the sales cycle," said Larry. "We missed the real problems, which culminated during the implementation and services phase."

Hargrove's perception was not good. Anna said Larry's company was interested only in the next sale and not in becoming a long-term player. In fact, Anna told Larry that his company was the last choice as they embarked on a plan to find a solutions provider for their sales-effectiveness software needs.

Larry decided to go back to the basics to better understand Anna's business. He decided to pinpoint the key influencers and Anna's business drivers. In short, he decided to take time up front to understand the buyer's perspective. Above all, he aimed to build an improved relationship whereby he could become a strategic adviser and partner.

"We realized that we couldn't continue to rush forward with this buyer. Either we would leave the buyer behind or they would leave us behind. We took a close look in our rearview mirror and saw the risk of Hargrove receding in the distance.

"We knew we had to collaborate with Anna's company and take time to understand her needs. Our experience was that we were being kept off Hargrove's team, and we knew that we had to take the time to develop a plan and an approach that would work for both of us—for us and for Hargrove.

"We knew we had to get their emotional buy-in. It was now or never. While we knew this would take more time in the beginning, we couldn't afford not to do it. And we knew that, subsequently, everything would flow smoother. Together we had to take on the task of solving the difficult problems in their organization, and together we had to define the steps that needed to be taken, when, and by whom."

The story has a happy ending, as you will learn in the coming chapters. Larry changed his company's approach.

By deciding to focus on Hargrove's business, Larry helped his company turn the corner.

Today, Anna has a different story to tell. "I never expected to say this," she told us, "but Outstanding Options has demonstrated their interest in our short- and long-term business success. I truly believe we are strategic partners."

Do you remember the fairy tale of the tortoise and the hare? Slow-and-steady wins the race. The same principle applies in buyer relationships. Going fast often results in arriving later, not sooner. Throughout *Selling for the Long Run*, you will learn strategies for slowing down so that you can win the race. Critical to this is the concept of collaborating, which can be done only when you sit calmly together on a Ferris wheel and avoid those roller coaster rides where no one is able to speak to or hear anyone else.

Bridging the Gap Through Collaboration

Collaborating with a buyer tears down a wall that the buyer has erected to stop sellers from taking advantage. Instead, it bridges the gap between the sales mentality and the buyer's mentality, aligning the two processes.

The strategic sales professional knows that going slowly is the only way to create a collaborative environment. By using a collaborative process, the sales professional can discover what the organization looks like, who reports to whom, and the company's business issues and priorities. Collaboration usually leads to fewer buyer objections, including objections related to price.

In short, collaboration creates stickiness.

Collaboration also creates competitive advantage in the post-sale period. Buyers are loyal to you for longer periods of time, making repeat business easier. You become the default vendor, not the obligatory provider invited to the party only for the required shopping or comparing phase of buying.

You hear about collaboration all the time these days, but an extensive amount of trepidation surrounds collaboration. People talk about collaboration positively, but when it comes time to implement collaboration procedures, businesses are overcome by anxiety. They wonder:

o What is collaboration really all about?
o How do we start collaborating with a buyer?
o Isn't it easier to let the buyers continue to play by their rules while we play by ours?
o How would we broach the subject with buyers?

As you continue through this book, I will introduce a number of collaborative tools that you can use with your buyers. But before I get to tools, let's take a few minutes to examine the basics of a collaborative relationship and why it is so critical.

Creating Collaboration

When we consider buying and selling, we tend to consider them as buying *versus* selling. In other words, we think of these concepts as polar opposites when, in fact, the buying *and* selling process should be a march toward the same goal.

The dynamics of buying and selling have been examined many times before, but historically, books, papers, and lectures usually address one or the other. Very rarely are they looked at as side-by-side activities, probably because they are considered to be two opposite and distinct processes.

Obviously, the key to a successful collaboration is to bridge the two. We need to answer the following questions:

○ How can we get the two closer together?
○ How can we make the buying and selling experience more fulfilling and predictable for both sides of the equation?

Let's take a look at buying *versus* selling, side by side, so that we can examine how and where perceptions and expectations get off track. Let's first look at the stages a buyer moves through when buying.

The Buyer's Process Visually, the buying process looks something like this:

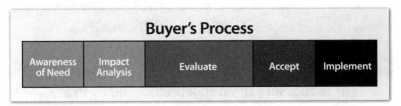

1. **The first stage that occurs is *awareness of need*.** An organization (or person) typically goes through a planning process to optimize its business for the upcoming year, quarter, or month and becomes aware of the needs it must address to meet its goals and objectives. Perhaps a system breaks down and requires the company to shift its priorities and address an urgent need. Perhaps the buyer realizes it could be more effective with a new technology. Perhaps the buyer is expanding its product range

and needs a vendor who can provide parts. Regardless, the buyer's first step is to become aware of its needs.

2. **The second stage involves *impact analysis.*** All unmet needs must be prioritized based on goals and objectives. What are the must-haves versus the nice-to-haves? What business impact will be made if the buyer has the need? The buyer ties priority to business results.

3. **Next, the buyer will *evaluate.*** Because multiple ways exist to address a need, the buyer will consider available alternatives and analyze the potential impact those alternatives would have on the business. Once an initial list of alternatives has been created, the buyer will take a closer look at each one so that it can more thoroughly assess and recommend an approach.

4. **Once the buyer has evaluated the alternatives, the buyer moves into the *accept* stage.** The buyer will validate what was evaluated through reference checks, site visits, proof of concepts, and the like. The buyer will negotiate price, contract terms, and follow the acceptance criteria set by the organization's policy.

5. **Finally, the buyer will *implement* the changes and begin to measure the impact.** Once the contracts are complete, the buyer incorporates the solution—expecting it will have a positive impact on the business.

Regardless of what a person is buying—whether it is a service or a product—this is the process he or she follows. For instance, consider the very basic and familiar process of moving:

1. First, as your family or your wealth changes, you identify that you need to move (awareness of need).

2. Then you analyze your options and what impact these different options will have on your quality of life and pocketbook. You could rent, buy a condo, or purchase a home. You could move in December or wait until the new year (impact analysis).
3. You next evaluate the neighborhoods and homes you have selected as your options (evaluate).
4. You select a home, take others to see the home to validate your selection, negotiate price and improvements, acquire funding, and sign the contracts (accept).
5. Finally, you begin the process of packing your belongings and moving into your new home (implement).

Now, let's take a look at what a typical sales process might look like.

The Sellers' Process Visually, the selling process looks something like this:

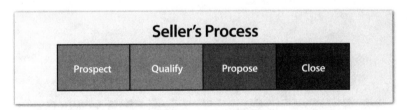

1. A sales team goes through *prospecting* whereby they define the activities needed to identify prospects that will generate revenue for the coming year (or quarter, month, fiscal period). Like the buyer, the seller is performing a planning process, but instead of becoming aware of a need, the seller is determining where to spend time to develop the best leads.

2. Once a lead is uncovered, the sales professional must *qualify* that lead, using criteria including, but not limited to, budget, time frame, and access to decision makers.
3. Once an opportunity is qualified, the seller moves on to *propose* that solution, which might include giving presentations and demonstrations and discussing pricing.
4. After proposing a solution and generating a proposal, the seller *closes* the sale by signing the contract. The deal is now complete, and the sales representative most likely moves on to focus on closing the next piece of business to make his or her defined quota.

Looking at the two processes side by side, they do not seem to be well aligned. In fact, the table on the next page details exactly how misaligned the processes are. Too often, the sellers' process is implemented in isolation from the buyers'. The buyers simply do not care about the sellers' process because

Buyer's Process				
Awareness of Need	Impact Analysis	Evaluate	Accept	Implement
Prospect	Qualify	Propose	Close	Seller is no longer involved
Seller's Process				

the buyers have the money. As such, the responsibility is on the sellers to make sure the two processes are aligned.

Buying and Selling: A Side-by-Side Analysis

THE BUYING PROCESS	THE SELLING PROCESS
While optimizing the business, the buyer becomes **aware of a need.**	While looking at the territory, the seller determines the activities necessary to identify a **prospect** and generate a lead.
The buyer determines the **impact** of the need and compares its priority to all other company needs.	The seller determines whether the prospect is **qualified** by asking a few questions: Does the buyer have a budget? Will the buyer buy this year? Do I have access to decision makers?
The buyer **evaluates** what options are available to solve the need.	The seller **proposes** the solution, ensuring that the buyer knows how wonderful the solution is.
The buyer **accepts** the identified solutions by validating what the buyer believes to be true, identifying any risks to implement, acquiring funding, negotiating price, defining contract terms, and gaining approvals.	The seller tries to **close** the deal by the end of the quarter by getting the contract signed.
The buyer **implements** the new solution and measures the impact.	The seller says good luck and moves on to the next opportunity.

Given our commitment to considering the buyer's perspective, let's look more closely at the differences in perspective so that we can truly understand what is going on in the minds of the buyers and sellers.

WHILE THE BUYER IS IN ONE STAGE...	THINKING...	THE SELLER IS IN A DIFFERENT STAGE...	THINKING...
Awareness of need	What is the business environment, and how are the market conditions? How do we optimize the business? What are our strategic planning goals, strategies, and initiatives?	Prospect	How big is my territory? Where do I begin? Where can I make quota? What resources do I need to cover my territory to make quota? What messages do I need to create a lead? What activities do I need to uncover to create opportunities?
Impact analysis	What is the potential business impact? How does this rank compared to other projects on the list? Do we need executive sponsors? What is the cost compared to the benefit?	Qualify	Do you have need? Do you fit my criteria? Do you like my message? Do you have a budget? Is there someone who can make a decision? Is this urgent? Will you buy now? How quickly can you make a decision? How large of an opportunity could this be?

Evaluate	We need to define the requirements. What is available? Do you really have something that can help me? How are other people solving this issue? I didn't know this was available. How are you different? What criteria should we use to evaluate you? Whom do we trust? You do not have my best interest at heart. You are interested only in getting the sale. What are your tricks or gimmicks? How do we protect our executives and control you?	Propose	How do I get access to your executives? *Who is my Coach?* (This concept will be explored in Chapter 4, "Influence Maps: Understanding the People Who Vote") Who are the decision makers? You need to see and hear our message. Your issues are the same as every other buyer I talk to. You buyers are always worried about the same things! I have the answer for you! I must control the situation. You just need to do what I tell you. I wish you buyers were smarter. You never tell me anything. You always have a gatekeeper in place.
Accept	Do you have the resources to make us successful? Is this the best deal? How much risk do we have, and how do we mitigate risk if we select you?	Close	Let's get the contract signed! I need to make my forecast. When do I get to move on to the next deal?
Implement	We can now begin the project. This is the beginning or our relationship. How do we make this thing work? How do we measure success?	Seller is no longer involved	Time to hand you off to a new team. This is the end of our relationship. Not my problem. Someone else in the company is now responsible for you. Good luck. See you next time we want to make a sale.

No wonder there is friction in the selling process and frustration in the buying process!

Bridging Buying with Selling

Collaboration creates Velcro between buying and selling, bridging the gap in such a way that both buyer and seller are reaching mutual goals. Most sales representatives have a sales process they work out in their head. Some may even have it in writing. Regardless, almost all of them keep this process a secret from their buyers.

But why?

The buyer knows that the seller has to make quota. In turn, the seller knows that the buyer has many opportunities to choose from and must compete for the win. What is the harm in collaborating during this joint process so that the buyer and seller can both make the best use of their time?

Let's look at an example.

Larry's company, Outstanding Options, has an official sales process used to forecast revenue and review opportunities. This formal process is used to measure the sales rep's progress in any given sales campaign. This sales process is considered an internal process and is never revealed or discussed outside of the Outstanding Options sales organization.

When Larry first joined the Outstanding Options team, the sales process had five basic stages:

1. Target
2. Qualify
3. Propose
4. Commit
5. Win!

This process was quite similar to the one described earlier in this chapter. However, it was worded in a way that was somewhat offensive to Larry's buyer, as if the seller were a hunter and the buyer the prey—with the seller's focus on achieving the trophy kill!

The truth of the matter is that most companies have a similar process, although the wording is not always identical. In fact, based on my work with more than forty thousand sales professionals, the sales processes are always similar to one another. The key to bridging buying with selling is to change the vocabulary so that the process is buyer-friendly and collaborative, addressing both the buyer's needs and the seller's needs. This way, the seller can share the process and create a collaborative environment.

When InfoMentis started working with Outstanding Options, we suggested that the company reword its sales process so that a sales representative, such as Larry, could openly discuss the process with buyers. Our suggestion was this:

1. Business development
2. Understand business challenge
3. Collaborate and validate
4. Collaborate and accept proposal
5. Implement and measure success

Sales representatives who adopt this language can be transparent about their company's process. A buyer would certainly expect Larry to look for business opportunities (business development). After all, the buyer is also looking to develop business. The buyer would certainly expect Larry to understand his buyer's business challenge so that he is spending time with people who need his solution; concurrently, the buyer is looking to align with a seller who offers a viable solution (understand business challenge). Understanding the business challenge presents the buyer with a friendly, non-manipulative term to which the buyer feels connected.

The buyer would also expect Larry to invest the time and energy to learn and/or discover enough so that he can collaborate on the right solution. Instead of simply jumping to the proposal, collaboration implies that the buyer will participate in the solution, thereby presenting a less offensive and more inviting option to the buyer (collaborate and validate solution). The buyer would also expect Larry to collaborate on the proposal and ask for some sort of commitment indicating acceptance of the solution presented. Concurrently, the buyer will be asking for a mutual commitment, which opens the door for the close (collaborate and accept proposal). And, of course, the buyer expects Larry to implement and measure success; likewise, the buyer also wants to close the evaluation process and begin the implementation of the new solution (implement and measure success).

Given that the buyer already expects these steps to occur, and that they are ordered and worded in a way that suggests the buyer is an equal player in the process, why wouldn't Larry create Velcro by sharing his process with the buyer? In doing so, he would create a series of positive outcomes. He would build the buyer's trust in Larry. Based on Larry's full disclosure of the process and willingness to spend time and energy learning about the buyer's business, the buyer will have the perception that Larry is:

○ A solid businessperson, not just a sales rep
○ Organized and methodical

- Interested in the buyer
- A good cultural fit
- Honest

The buyer would expect Larry to:

- Communicate expectations around collaboration and working together
- Communicate that he will not waste anyone's time
- Set expectations with the buyer and invite the buyer to set expectations of Larry and his team
- Insert reality into the process as it relates to time frames and effort

In addition to sharing the stages, Larry could set milestones with the buyer to make sure the buyer and seller are in the same place at the same time. Consider what Larry's script might look like:

When working with clients, we have found that we usually go through a five-stage process when evaluating a potential solution. First, we look for business opportunities, just like any company. When we've found what might be a good fit, we make sure that we understand the business challenge and that our goals are mutually aligned. This is what we are doing right now. I want to make sure that we both feel that our solution would address your business challenge so that we are both spending our time wisely. I don't want to waste your time, so I want to make sure that we are aligned with any potential business challenge that we may identify and you are able to justify the invest-ment of time and resources to evaluate a solution.

Next, we want to collaborate on validating the possible solution. This allows us to invest time and resources in understanding your business and your needs so that you and I can collaborate on the solution and make sure that our solution will be applied appropriately to your company. Of course, I'll deliver a demonstration and give you a taste of what the solution will look like so that you can make a decision. Before we go through the efforts of submitting a proposal, we want to make sure that the solution meets your business challenge, so during this phase, we'll be collaborating to make sure that what I am recommending is right for you. At the end of this phase, I will submit a proposal.

At that point, assuming all goes well, we will both be ready to accept the terms and expectations of the proposal. If you are comfortable with my solution, we'll work together, get the agreements in place, and begin the last phase, which is when we implement the process, and then make sure we are measuring success. It's important to note that this phase never ends as long as you are using our solution or service. We want to make sure that you have standards by which you can consistently evaluate the solution we propose.

Now, this is the typical process, which is what I have found to work well with my clients in the past. If it is OK with you, I would really like to understand your process and how you have gone about evaluating solutions in the past so that we both have all the right expectations. Again, I want to make sure that we are both on the same page as we move forward. With that in mind, what would you change about the process I just outlined?

Bridging the gap requires that the seller change its stages to align with the buyer's stages and enable the collaborative environment to exist.

Milestones

Changing and aligning the stages are not enough. The seller must also insert milestones into the process so that the seller and buyer can come together to measure progress and continually ensure that both are at the same place at the same time. A milestone represents a specific point in time within the process at which buyer and seller come together to make sure they want to advance in the process. Importantly, the milestone should be verifiable, meaning the seller can witness the buyer performing the verifiable outcome.

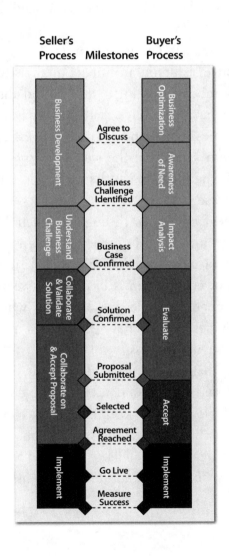

In the previous graphic, we see how these two processes are not only aligned but also verified via milestones. While the buyer is analyzing need, the seller is developing business by beginning to understand the buyer's business and determining whether the seller's solution is appropriate for the buyer. To transition to the next stage, the seller asks the buyer's team to discuss their progress—a milestone allowing them to decide whether the buyer has a need that the seller might be able to address.

The processes will continue to move forward in tandem. While the buyer is doing an impact analysis of the various solutions, the seller is working to qualify and align the buyer. The seller can assist the buyer with the impact analysis and, at the same time, qualify and align objectives. The seller and buyer will both know that the stage was successfully completed if and when they reach the next milestone—defining the business case.

The process continues throughout each of the stages, allowing buyer and seller to come together to create a solution that will solve the buyer's business challenge. When this format is followed, the gap is bridged between buyers and sellers; in essence, the seller has a map by which to choose the right activities that will have the greatest impact in aligning with the buying process.

Be aware that creating a collaborative environment is often easier said than done. Skeptical by nature, sellers assume that buyers want to keep their cards close to the vest, so many sellers have little interest in collaboration. In fact, most of them hear about collaboration and think: *Our buyers would never share that information with us!*

But is this true? Will they refuse to share information with you, or have you failed to ask? You won't know until you try.

Getting the buyer to engage or collaborate is all about taking the first step toward collaboration and walking the walk—not just talking the talk. You must invite the buyer to play and be prepared to demonstrate and talk about why collaborating is valuable to them (not you). This means that you may need to share more with the buyer than you normally do, showing the buyer your cards and how your process will benefit the buyer.

If you do the right thing, the money will come. If you are working to help the buyer, the buyer will become your customer. The "right thing" requires that you explain to your buyer what happens within your organization at each step, what resources might be required, and how you plan to use these resources to bring value to the buyer.

The difference between sellers who sell and sellers who only dream of selling is their answer to these questions: "Do you get up every morning and ask yourself, *What am I going to sell today?* Or do you get up every morning and ask yourself, *How am I going to help someone today?*" Top producers ask the latter.

PART 2

DETERMINING YOUR STRATEGY (WITHOUT A SILVER BULLET)

Most sales professionals want to jump straight into the sales strategy. Unfortunately, they spend too little time getting to know their buyer's business challenges, its key influencers, and its competitive landscape, all information that is necessary before the seller can pick a strategy.

In the previous chapter, we introduced a collaborative sales process that includes the buyer's perception and buyer participation in the stages and milestones through collaboration. Once the seller and buyer both understand the process, they must start engaging in the process.

Early on, both buyer and seller start thinking about how they are going to win. The buyer wants to win the most effective, least expensive solution. The seller wants to win the buyer's business. But before the seller can set a strategy on how it might win, it must understand all the determinants of the strategy it ultimately selects. Namely, the seller must understand the following:

1. **The buyer's business situation or challenge** (as discussed in Chapter 3, "Collaboration Maps: Understanding Your Buyer's Business"). Understanding the business's needs gives you insight into what you can position as a potential solution, as well as the urgency and significance of the challenge.

2. **The people who vote** (discussed in Chapter 4, "Influence Maps: Understanding the People Who Vote"). The "people who vote" are the buyer's key influencers, the ones who are primarily responsible for driving strategy. These are the people who will make the buying decisions. To select the right strategy, we must know who these people are and what relationship they have to the business.

3. **The competitive landscape** (the subject of Chapter 5, "Competitive Maps: Understanding the Competitive Landscape"). The competitive landscape connects the business challenge and the people who vote by providing insight into how the seller's potential solution compares to any alternative solution from the perspective of the people who vote. The seller's opinion of the competitive advantages is not nearly as important as the buyer's opinion of the competitive advantages. Understanding the people who vote and the business challenge allows the seller to assess the competitive landscape. If all the people who vote believe that one seller's potential solution is significantly superior to any alternative, the seller will choose a Frontal Strategy; if only one or two on the buyer's ten-person team are convinced of a solution's superiority, the seller should choose a Flanking Strategy. I will discuss both of these strategies in Chapter 6, "Using Maps to Pick Your Strategy."

Only once you understand and analyze these three components are you in a position to finally select the strategy.

CHAPTER 3

Collaboration Maps

Understanding Your Buyer's Business

> "People don't care how much you know until they know how much you care."
> —Theodore Roosevelt, twenty-sixth president of the United States

E arlier, we talked about how the sales professionals are perceived. Buyers perceive that sellers are constantly forgetting about the eye of the buyer and ignoring the buyer's point of view entirely. The top complaint we hear from buyers is this:

"The reason we didn't buy from vendor X is because they didn't understand our business." (as reported by InfoMentis during a win/loss analysis)

When a buyer has this perception, he feels shortchanged, as though he is not getting enough attention.

In fact, this perception is not entirely accurate. The seller is focused on moving a sale forward, meeting quotas, relieving pressure from management, and eliminating the competition. The seller has too many pressures and feels that she lacks the time or resources to divert focus away from these concerns.

The reality, however, is that sellers cannot afford to continue doing business the old way, whereby the buyer feels that the seller does not care about his goals or objectives. The buyer interprets this behavior as arrogance, and sellers and service professionals who appear to be self-focused pay the price through lost opportunities and unhappy buyers.

o Approximately 92 percent of executives say that "initial sales calls are of *little or no value*," according to SiriusDecisions.

o The same report found that 82 percent of sales executives indicated salespeople *"have not done their homework* in regards to [the buyer's] critical issues or needs."

o And 71 percent indicate "salespeople *talk too much about their company* and products and not enough about [the buyer]."

Because of silver bullet syndrome, the seller fails do the right thing for the buyer. The seller does not take the time to look at the situation from the buyer's perspective, which can lead to a long sales cycle fraught with miscommunications, misunderstandings, and expectations that fail to relate to the buyer's needs. Many times the buyer is left to determine how to apply the solution, which may or may not fit.

Ignoring the buyer's perspective is like a boomerang—it feels good when you throw it, but if you are not paying attention, the boomerang will come back and hit you in the form of postponed decisions, tough negotiations, and lost deals. Those buyers who do accept your solution will likely feel buyers' remorse or perceive you as a misleading or dishonest seller. Any of these boomerang effects can potentially damage or ruin your relationship with the buyer.

My friend and colleague recently experienced this boomerang effect when she was learning to fly an airplane. Flying is a quiet and peaceful and beautiful experience, but then comes the landing. A big milestone in flying is the first solo. Immediately, my friend realized that she did not want to screw up the landing in her first solo flight (or in *any* flight, for that matter).

She practiced and practiced for the solo landing—experiencing a multitude of poor attempts resulting in one bumpy landing after another. She did not have a breakthrough until her instructor said something that clicked:

The success of your landing is dependent upon all of the things that you do to set up the landing. Your altitude and speed at different points during your approach will determine your landing, as well as whether you are stable as you manage the final approach.

As in flying, the combination of slow and steady in a sales transaction makes the "crescendo event" successful. If you pay attention before the "landing" (the close), setting up the transaction right, you will have much better success. But if you start by taking shortcuts during the sales cycle, you are more likely to have a lot of recovering to do as you transition your client from buyer to customer. You might even crash.

Mapping for Collaboration

Throughout this book, we will discuss a number of useful collaboration tools that allow you to earn the right to advance with your buyer while checking to ensure that you and the buyer are on the same page and working at the same pace. One classic sales mistake occurs when the sales team believes it has advanced in the sales process because it performed all the planned activities only to learn that the buyer has not advanced at the same pace.

How does that happen?

The buyer and seller find themselves on different pages when the seller fails to check the pace of advancement.

As we discussed in earlier chapters, collaborative tools are extremely useful to help verify that the buyer and the seller are at the same place at the same time.

Perhaps one of the most important tools in setting the stage for a collaborative environment is a Collaboration Map. The Collaboration Map serves as a tool that allows you to confirm with the buyer that you "get it," that you understand the business challenge the buyer has described to you, allowing the buyer to collaborate and offer additional information that you might be missing or may have misunderstood.

The key to collaboration is to make the process visual. The buyer will never read a thirty-two-page report, whereas a picture instantly speaks a thousand words. The Collaboration Map serves as a visual representation of the buyer's business challenges and instantly changes the buyer's perception of the seller. The buyer begins to understand that you, the seller, are more interested in what the buyer needs than in talking about yourself. This can be the first step in earning the right to advance with the buyer.

Successful use of a Collaboration Map has several important outcomes.

1. First, this tool allows the buyer and seller to determine if they have potential to do business.
2. The Collaboration Map is also one of the first ways that a seller can prove that he or she has an understanding of the buyer's business challenges.
3. Finally, Collaboration Maps serve as guidelines for staying focused on the buyer's perspective by reminding the seller of the issues, concerns, and objectives that a solution must address.

Let's look at a Collaboration Map. The following map represents typical challenges facing sales organizations today and can be used for early discussion in the sales cycle.

Let's say that Larry is calling on Anna of Hargrove, a telecommunications organization. While he knows that no two organizations are exactly alike, he also knows that business challenges, initiatives, and concerns trend by industry. Larry might draw from industry experience—as well as sources such as Hoover's, One Source, analyst reports, and earnings calls—to begin understanding the factors that influence the goals of the organization, which might include government regulations, competition, and suppliers.

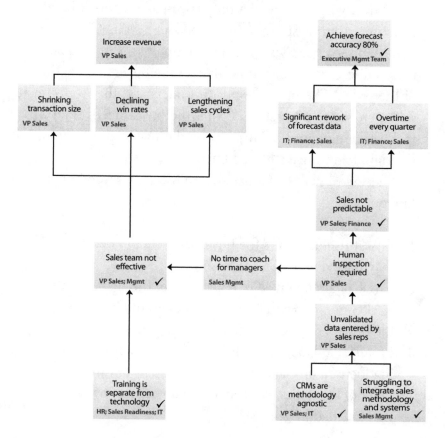

Larry can then create the beginnings of a Collaboration Map to guide his first conversation with Anna. The conversation might sound something like this:

Anna, as I have worked with other organizations in the telecom industry and researched a bit about your own company, I have come to understand that many of the challenges with sales team effectiveness and sales predictability discussed on your last analyst call are common across the industry. In fact, many IT organizations are struggling with how to integrate sales methodologies and systems effectively. Typically, training is separate from technology, customer relationship management systems are methodology-agnostic, and human inspection is still a major requirement to get an accurate forecast. IT has been working hard to try to fix the sales insight challenge. Your organization has certainly looked at this, given your current initiative to find a sales force automation solution. What has your team discovered to be the major challenges or barriers with sales force effectiveness here at Hargrove?

Anna might agree with the common industry challenges on Larry's map, or she may have entirely different challenges, or the map may have raised some issues that she had not previously considered. But one way or another, the map opens the conversation while allowing Larry to exhibit experience and knowledge of the business and IT challenges that exist with sales force automation. This also serves to open up the conversation with Anna in order to really understand what is going on within her organization.

As Larry listens to Anna's response, he takes notes on the Collaboration Map as she speaks. Anna has concrete knowledge that Larry is listening to her and incorporating her perspective.

If your organization can make Collaboration Maps part of its sales readiness training, you not only have a great starting point for early conversations with buyers, but you also have an accelerated process for new and existing sales team members. Having a sample Collaboration Map that showcases the issues or challenges your solution solves in the industry allows you to create a physical representation of the buyer's potential challenges and provides the basis for gathering additional information quickly by asking the right questions. A Collaboration Map increases and improves a team's knowledge of an industry and forces the seller to pay attention to the eye of the buyer.

As you start engaging the buyer in a business discussion about the industry, the buyer will naturally open up and share information with you. As the dialogue progresses, the buyer will likely share ownership in helping you complete the Collaboration Map, which is the first step in creating a collaborative environment.

Anna's response to Larry's question—"What has your team discovered to be the major challenges or barriers with sales force effectiveness here at Hargrove?"—reveals more about the company:

We get lots of requests from our sales and marketing teams about customer and competitive data that we just don't have. We hear complaints from the sales reps about our customer relationship management system's slow speed, difficulty of use, and lack of valuable information. The amount of overtime that our IT staff has to work— especially around quarter-end—to try to get sales management the information they need is frustrating. We spend a lot of time and resources looking at which technology platform decisions are good for the organization and will help us stay competitive. In addition, we have limited experience with this type of technology and how to integrate it into the business.

The beginning of Larry's Collaboration Map would look like this:

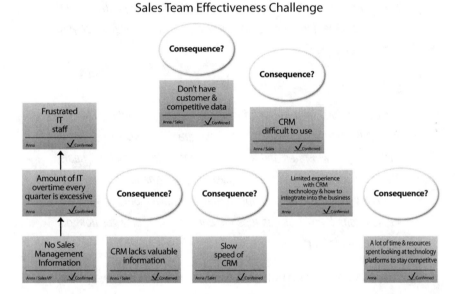

Sales Team Effectiveness Challenge

Some of Anna's issues had a cause-and-effect relationship. For instance, the overtime and high work requirements during quarter-end were causing employee frustration. However, she does not state what consequences the company has suffered as a result of the platform decisions that require too much time and too many resources. She also doesn't mention the consequences of the slow speed of the customer relationship management (CRM) system or the lack of valuable information for the sales reps. This reflects a gap in Larry's knowledge.

As you begin using Collaboration Maps, you will notice that the maps will always have gaps. This is not only acceptable but also useful in helping lead ongoing conversations.

69

You can use the gaps to frame your next questions, whether they occur in the same conversation or in later conversations.

Larry created the previous map from just one statement provided by Anna. In reality, the conversation would continue. Larry might ask:

> You mentioned technology choices and staying competitive. What types of competitive impact have you experienced because of your current technology?

Imagine that Anna's response is this:

> Our competitors seem to be bringing new and improved solutions to their sales teams more quickly than we are. We have seen a slight decline in our win rates and a larger decline in the size of our deals. We are suspicious that the sales cycle has lengthened but we don't know why. Our customers complain that they have more knowledge of our solutions than our sales reps do, and the value they get from our sales teams is limited.

Now Larry's map starts to fill out (see the following page).

Advancing

How do you know how many questions to ask? When do you have enough information captured to illustrate that you have earned the right to advance forward with the seller?

A seller has earned the right to move forward when he can identify the business's challenges and can tie his solution to something that is broken. This might seem straightforward, but let's take a look at these two criteria one at a time.

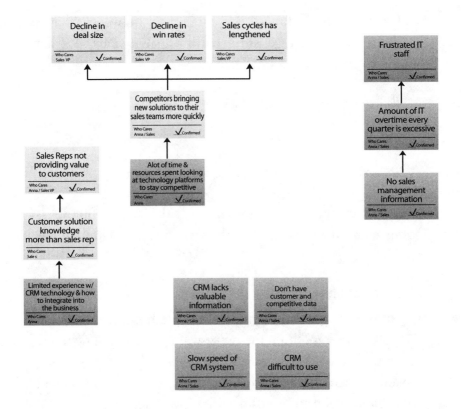

Challenges

Earlier defined sales methodologies have referred to a buyer's "pains" or "problems" and suggest that by solving these pains or problems you will win the deal. Nonetheless, I would encourage you to advance your thinking to that of the buyer. Buyers think in terms of "challenges" (a grouping of pains or problems) when discussing their business. Therefore, by understanding a buyer's business challenges you reveal a number of pains or problems that need to be resolved. However, it is important to remember that your potential value is tied to the buyer's business challenges and not to an individual pain or problem.

Imagine, for instance, the difference between what a seller might say if discussing pains versus what the seller might say if discussing challenges.

What are the pains I can solve for you?

versus

How can our solution help you overcome your challenges?

The former sounds as though the sales representative is going to fly in and save the day, whereas the latter builds collaboration.

Fixing the Broken

It is important to tie the solution to something that is broken as opposed to something the buyer wants or needs. The buyer can always change his wants and desires, but if something broken is needed today, it needs to be fixed today, and it will continue to need to be fixed tomorrow. Therefore, to secure your position in creating a possible solution, attach your solution to something that is broken. This was the fundamental thought of pain. However, when you advance your thinking to that of the buyer, you recognize that not all pains are equal.

When creating your Collaboration Map, there are different levels of "broken" or "pain." A task, situation, or process could be broken. This is the Tactical Pain (TP). Before moving forward, the sales representative must have identified and noted the consequences of the Tactical Pains in the Collaboration Map. The Tactical Consequences, known as Consequential Pains (CPs), are valid when they pertain to any of the following:

○ Financial consequence
○ Internal consequence
○ Strategic consequence
○ Political consequence

Buyers will pay large sums of money to make financial, internal, strategic, or political consequences disappear.

Earlier, Anna relayed to Larry that her company's platform decisions require too much time and too many resources. To improve this Tactical Pain and uncover the consequences, Larry can ask how much time Hargrove spends and how many resources it uses so that he can quantify the challenge and place a financial consequence on it. Anna also tells Larry that Hargrove is slow to bring new and improved solutions to market. Is this a strategic consequence? Political? Financial? Internal? It might even be all four! And if Larry continues to ask questions that show other consequences, such as the loss of revenue or impact on forecast, the Collaboration Map will begin to illustrate a clear path for questions that will ultimately reveal the Key Business Requirements (KBRs) of the decision maker and the business challenges that are preventing her from achieving her KBRs. Understanding the big picture makes the buyer comfortable, earning the seller the right to move forward.

Your Collaboration Map, therefore, is complete when it accomplishes the following:

1. It has identified the Tactical Pains.
2. It has identified the strategic, financial, internal, and/or political consequences of unresolved tactical pains.

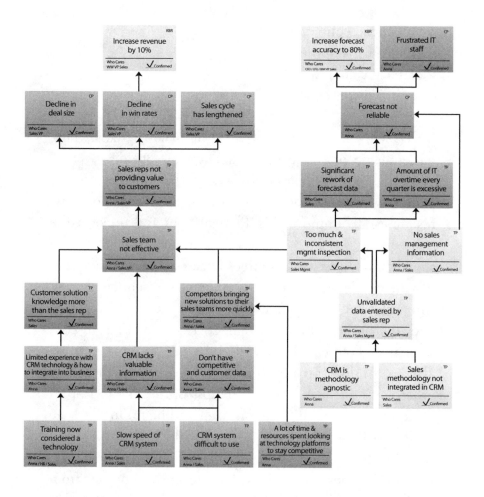

3. It has connected the challenges into a story.
4. It has identified the Key Business Requirements, which are the business requirements of the decision maker in the deal.

When the Tactical Pains the buyer has described are connected to strategic, financial, internal, or political consequences and are quantified so the buyer has a sense of magnitude or urgency, the Collaboration Map has earned the seller the right to move forward.

If, on the other hand, the business challenge is not attached to any issue of consequence, the seller must ask himself these questions:

○ *Am I talking to the right person? Who else might know more of the story?* In the next chapter, we will discuss how Influence Mapping can help a seller answer these two questions.

○ *If no consequence exists, why would the buyer move forward with my solution?* A buyer who cannot identify an impact is likely wasting your time.

Here are the key points to remember when building your Collaboration Map:

1. **Start with a hypothesis.** You and your company have created solutions to serve specific market needs. Those market needs are created because something was broken and needs to be fixed, or it doesn't exist and needs to be enabled. Start by creating a hypothesis that guesses what was broken or needed. Use that hypothesis as a starting point to begin your Collaboration Map and exhibit your industry or market expertise.

2. **Use planned High-Yield Questions to arrive at a more complete picture.** In later chapters, we will discuss High-Yield Questions, which uncover how the buyer's actual needs differ from your hypothesis. High-Yield Questions stimulate a business discussion with the buyer, allowing you to uncover clues about how you

might be able to help this client. Chapter 9, "High-Yield Questions to Support Your Strategy," discusses how to create High-Yield Questions, which become particularly important when you think about the balance of time and information relative to the buyer interaction. High-Yield Questions are a technique used to obtain the most insight in the least amount of time.

3. **Be careful of assumptions.** When creating a Collaboration Map, be careful not to transpose your assumed information into confirmed information. Make sure that what you believe to be true is actually true by verifying the challenges identified with the buyers. In each box of the map, note the persons who confirmed information so that you can easily see what has been confirmed versus what you have assumed. Assumed information is acceptable as long as you eventually confirm that it is true or use it to generate a discussion about the company's actual needs. If unconfirmed, assumptions are dangerous; if you use them as a tool to drive more face time with the buyer or showcase your knowledge of the business, they can be handy.

4. **Use tactical and consequential categories to guide you.** A buyer will not really care (and certainly will not score you on) whether you get everything right. However, sellers need to know if they have enough information to assess whether the solution will help the buyer. They also need to know if they have asked enough questions to understand the impact and to assure the right business results if the solution is implemented. Separate Tactical Pains from Consequential Pains so that you ask enough questions to capture the complete picture. Remember, challenges without visible business

consequences are probably not something that an organization will spend time and money to fix.

5. **Collaborate or share what you learn.** Breaking the habit of keeping a sales tool confined to your internal team can be difficult; however, a Collaboration Map is a much more powerful tool when shared with the buyer because you have validation that you listened well. The Collaboration Map communicates that you heard the buyer, and it allows the buyer fill in the gaps and make corrections if you have heard your client incorrectly or if you are missing key points. This makes the buyer part of your team.

6. **Use the Collaboration Map as a filter.** After you have verified that you are solving the right business challenges, you should use the Collaboration Map as your solution filter. As you are assembling your solution or deciding which customer success stories to tell or which references you may use, or which analyst and industry endorsements you may share with the buyer, you should use your map as your guideline for staying focused on what will resonate with this particular buyer, since your map should reflect this buyer's business challenges.

CHAPTER 4

Influence Maps

Understanding the People Who Vote

> "Treat a person as he is, and he will remain as he is. Treat him as he could be, and he will become what he should be."
> —Jimmy Johnson, former American football coach and analyst on "Fox NFL Sunday"

We've looked at Collaboration Maps as a way to represent the cause-and-effect relationships of key issues and challenges within an organization. We also looked at the importance of identifying those who "own" issues and challenges so that we are able to attach specific people to the buyer's challenges. With that in mind, we need to understand how much influence each person on the buying team has; as well, we need to identify other influencers who would impact a buying decision. We do this through Influence Maps.

GAINING PREFERENCE

An Influence Map is a visual representation of the people involved in or able to influence a buying decision. Influence Maps help you understand who influences the buying decision, who you have on your side, and with whom you need to spend some time. Influence Mapping is a powerful way to structure and examine information about the people involved in the buyer's decision-making process.

Influence Maps provide the following benefits:

○ They give you a clear picture of the key players and their spheres of influence. Influence Maps provide more than simply the structure of an organization—they identify the people who actually have the most influence on a decision. Though it might seem that key executives are always the influencers, this is often not the case. Often, a decision is delegated to a line employee, one who works "in the trenches" of the organization. A respected line employee with an area of expertise might provide more input into a final decision than an executive.

○ They illustrate what you know and do not know about the people involved in the buying decision, including their preference toward your solution.

○ They help you identify a buyer who might also be acting as your Coach, which we describe later in this chapter.

○ They compress the time it takes for your team to understand influence, validate information, and plan collaboratively.

○ They demonstrate whether the challenges identified in the Collaboration Map are tied to people of influence. If they are not, you might need to uncover some new business challenge that is tied to people of influence. After all, if the people of influence have no stake in the challenges the solution addresses, why would they move forward?

As with Collaboration Maps, early Influence Maps will have more gaps in information than complete information. The people represented early in the sales process might include a couple of people you have met with, along with key people who you have identified from the buyer's website who might be important to contact. An early Influence Map might have only one name.

81

Basic Elements

Just as with a Collaboration Map, the information that you complete on the Influence Map will evolve over time. As you begin to learn more about the people who are involved in or influence a decision, the Influence Map allows you to track what you know about the influencers within an organization, as well as the things you must learn. We put this information into six basic categories.

1. **Name and title of each individual.** Having both is important. Calling the CIO is tough if you do not know her name. Calling on Anna Morrison without realizing she is the vice president of information technologies is embarrassing.

2. **Each person's role in the evaluation.** Be able to answer these questions about all the people on the map:
   ○ What are their roles in the evaluation?
   ○ Are they the decision makers, the executive sponsors, the Coaches, the technical buyers, the end users, the project managers, the financial analysts?

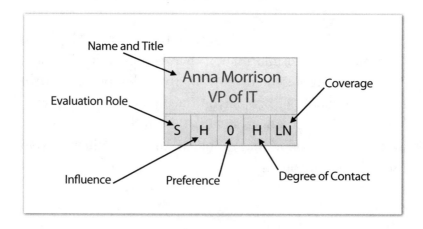

A seller should create a standardized language to describe the roles of buyers so that a common lexicon can be used for team discussions. For instance, the different roles might be represented as follows:

C = Coach

DM = Decision maker

G = Gatekeeper

R = Recommender

S = Sponsor

I recommend that the seller identify a Coach within the buying team in all cases. A Coach is someone on the buying team who has high preference for your solution and *wants you to win,* no different from a football coach. In fact, if you cannot identify a Coach from the buying team, you might not be able to win. Using the Influence Map to help you decide whether anyone on the buying team is on your side is a good way to take an early indicator of whether you should continue to fight for the sale.

3. **Each person's level of influence.** Some people's opinions carry more weight than others, and some are more willing to use their influence than others. Let's not ignore the fact that some people cannot say *yes* but can say *no.*

   Assess influence by doing the following:

   o Observe customer actions on conference calls, during group meetings, or during one-on-one meetings. Ask yourself:

     * *Do others turn to this person for advice?* If so, the person has high influence.

     * *Do others pay attention to or ignore this person when speaking?*

- Ask questions about past projects to reveal influence. For instance:
  - "Who drove the previous or any similar evaluation?" Influential people are also responsible for multiple projects.
  - "What would you have done differently on the last project?" Influential people will answer this question with more autonomy.
  - "What were the reasons you were successful with previous projects?"
  - "Whom would you want on this project to make it successful?"
  - "What is the best way to get things done in your organization?"
  - "How was the decision made in other projects?"
  - "What is the process to evaluate, and who should be involved?"
- Test the buyers with the results on certain tasks to determine the influence. For instance, is the person able to gain access to an executive?

Assessing all of these things—as well as any other actions that indicate whether a person has high, medium, or low influence—is critical. Just because someone says he or she has influence doesn't make it true. You need to test for influence and witness some actions that demonstrate influence.

In indicating a person's influence, you can use the following key code:

H = High influence

M = Medium influence

L = Low influence

4. **Each person's preference.** Your Influence Map should note each person's preference. Does he or she prefer you? Prefer an alternative? Or is he or she neutral? Following are some signs that a person has preference for you, your competitor, or no one.

A PERSON WHO PREFERS YOUR SOLUTION . . .	A PERSON WHO PREFERS A COMPETITOR'S SOLUTION . . .	A PERSON WHO IS NEUTRAL . . .
Provides you with confidential information.	Always initiates discussions about problems with your solution.	Shows no interest in the solution's success or failure.
Provides advantage to you and not others.	Is generally uncooperative.	Tries to treat all equally until a preference is determined.
Collaborates with you on how to win.	Creates barriers.	
Introduces you to all the key decision makers.	Asks menacing or off-topic questions.	
Supports your solution in public.		
Alerts you to potential barriers.		

If your Coach has preference for you, be sure you can identify specific actions he or she has demonstrated that would indicate such preference.

Preference is an important aspect to gauge early in the process because:

○ You could have someone of high influence with preference for the alternative, and this will affect the strategy you choose, as we will discuss in Chapter 6, "Using Maps to Pick Your Strategy."

○ Preference combined with influence is a powerful combination and could earn you the right to advance.

When you combine influence and preference, you will have a very clear idea of what needs to be covered by your sales team. For example, you may have someone on the buying team with high influence with preference for the competitor. This person might be the competitor's Coach. By identifying this person, you can evaluate the competitor's Coach's influence in comparison to your own Coach's influence. Perhaps your Coach has more influence over key executives. Perhaps the competitor's Coach has more influence, in which case you should develop a plan to neutralize the competitor's Coach, or you should develop a second Coach (or even multiple Coaches). This is the power of an Influence Map—you know where to spend your time and what your actions should be.

Preference on an Influence Map can be indicated as follows:

+ = Favors your solution

0 = Neutral

− = Favors alternative

5. **Degree of contact.** How much time have you spent with this person, relative to all the time you have spent with the buyer? Sellers can categorize their degree of contact as high, medium, or low. Many times, your Influence Map will tell you that the sales team is spending a majority of time with people of low or medium influence instead of with decision makers or Coaches. As well, most sellers spend time with buyers they believe

have preference for the seller. Make sure you are spending the majority of your time with people of influence and that you are trying to shift preference to you.

You can indicate degree of contact on an Influence Map as follows:

H = High contact

M = Moderate contact

N = No contact

L = Low contact

6. **Coverage.** Who is going to cover this buyer? In team selling environments, assigning coverage sets the team's expectations properly and allows sellers to grasp all opportunities to develop the right relationships with buyers. Especially in larger, more complex sales situations, sellers might have to divide and conquer. When we see large buying teams and coverage is all carried by one sales rep, we can see that this is not realistic, nor does it leverage the talents of the entire team. Instead, we try to divvy responsibilities, noting which person on the seller's team is responsible by inserting his or her initials in the bottom-right box of the Influence Map.

With this in mind, consider how to read this section of an Influence Map. We can tell that Anna Morrison, the vice president of information technologies, is the executive sponsor. While her degree of influence is high, she still has no preference for any of the sellers missing high contact. Larry Neil is responsible for "covering" her.

Normally, this would not be considered positive because a person with high contact should have preference by now.

In Anna's case, though, her preference indicates a positive shift. Remember that during her initial meeting with Larry, she told him he was her last choice. By paying attention to the eye of the buyer, Larry has actually made a tremendous amount of progress. Knowing this tells us that Larry should continue his course of action with Anna, asking her more questions to understand what is important to her and continuing to move her preference in his favor.

Let's say that, during the course of Larry's meeting, he has had a chance to spend time with Anna and her colleagues. Based upon what he has learned so far, he currently thinks that the Influence Map looks something like this:

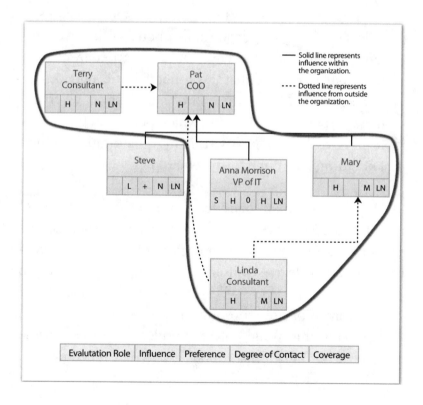

From this depiction, Larry can see that the people he has spent time with are Anna and Steve. Coverage with Anna is good, though she still does not prefer the solution. Larry realizes he might need to work on High-Yield Questions (see Chapter 9) so that he can uncover why Anna has not embraced his solution.

After spending considerable time with Steve, Larry decides that Steve has low influence, so he does not want to focus too much more time on Steve. Three other people have high influence—one with whom Larry has had no contact, and two with whom Larry has had little contact. As well, he does not know whether Terry has high or low influence because Larry and Terry have spent little time together. From this Influence Map, it appears that Larry needs to put together a plan to get some time with Mary, Linda, Terry, and Pat. He also needs to find a Coach on the buying team.

Building Your Influence Map

As you begin to build your Influence Map, some of the gaps in information will be fairly obvious. You will have blocks you simply do not know how to label. If you are a taskmaster, you might be inclined to quickly complete the task of building an Influence Map by filling in all empty boxes quickly, based on your gut reaction alone. Remember, though, that an Influence Map is a tool to help you learn influence, not a task you can simply cross off your list. You are looking for actions that the buyer performs that will provide you with information about the buyer's influence, preference, and role so that you will not have to rely on simply your opinion. The Influence Map is a dynamic work in progress that will accompany you through all stages of the sales process.

Develop a "To-Do List"

To maintain the integrity of the Influence Map, create a system of checks and balances whereby you ask yourself the following question before filling in a block: *How do I know?* If, for instance, you are preparing to categorize Anna as someone of high influence, you might ask: *How do I know? What has Anna done that would indicate high influence?*

You will observe from your map that you can start to create a "to-do list" based on your knowledge of certain key factors.

Outside Influencers Employees might not be the only influencers on a buying team. Consultants for or professional peers of a business might influence a buying decision. If your company sells computer networks, a technician whom the buying team calls any time it needs its network updated will certainly influence the buyer's decision, even if the technician is an independent contractor not employed by the buyer. Your Influence Map should identify such influencers, their role, degree of influence, and preference. If an outside person has influence, make sure someone "covers" the influencer as part of your strategy to create preference for your solution.

Your Assessments As you begin to categorize individuals of influence, refrain from relying too heavily on just one person's opinion. You might be tempted to rely exclusively on guidance from an ally within the organization, but remember that a person who is friendly and kind does not necessarily prefer your solution. A person might like you tremendously while still preferring another organization's solution. Remember Jim Hall, the seasoned sales professional who was liked by all? He lost many of his loyal clients to a competitor with a nasty temperament because Jim relied too heavily on his assessment of how his clients felt about him.

Before relying on people within an organization, test their preference, again by asking, *How do I know?* An employee who speaks positively of your solution to others on the evaluation team and defends your solution to others might very well have preference for your solution. A person who speaks positively of you, but not your solution, might prefer the competition.

Beware, as well, of assuming that someone is your Coach. If a person gives you information about the buyer's needs, he or she might simply be friendly and helpful. If a person coaches you on how to win a deal and creates competitive advantages for you, the person might be your Coach. If you think you have identified a Coach, test your assessment by making sure the person is helping you gain an advantage over your competition. Here's what a coach might do for you:

o Tell you how to win
o Tell you who your enemies are and how to overcome or neutralize them
o Tell you if you are winning or losing the deal
o Work with you proactively
o Collaborate with you on a plan to support your progress

In short, if you cannot answer the assessment question— How do I know?—then you have an action item for your to-do list.

A Team's Balance Regardless of what your kindergarten teacher might have told you, everyone is not the same. Not all opinions are equal, and levels of influence vary among employees. As well, degree of influence often toggles among several people. If a company is considering buying a benefits package, a human resources director might be highly influential, whereas the human resources director's opinion about a technology solution might be totally disregarded.

If your Influence Map does not reflect this diversification, instead assigning all executives as highly influential and all line employees as not-at-all influential, you likely are missing the big picture. If the majority of the people on your Influence Map have both preference for you and high influence but you have not closed the deal, something is amiss. If you have identified only people with low influence, you likely will not close the deal unless you start speaking with people of higher influence.

Accuracy

Remember this key rule when making an Influence Map: you are far better off leaving something blank than listing misinformation. If you have had little to no contact with someone, you will have a difficult time assessing his or her influence and preference. You may understand his or her role, name, and title, but you must dig deeper to understand his or her influence and preference. Until you have the time to do that, leaving a space blank simply indicates that you have an action item for your to-do list.

Because influence and political dynamics are sensitive areas, putting time and thought into the individuals with whom you are interacting is critical. You have only a limited amount of time to determine this information, so you cannot spend hours learning everything about everyone. Clearly, a well-defined plan of attack allows you to understand the high influencers so you can spend time with those who have the greatest impact on the decision.

When completing your Influence Map, ask yourself these questions:

o *Are these really the only people who will make this decision?*
o *Who are the outside influencers?*
o *How have they made decisions of this kind in the past, and who has been involved?*
o *What would prevent them from moving forward?*
o *Who else does this decision impact in the organization?*
o *Who can say no?*
o *Why would I lose?*

Ask High-Yield Questions

One of the keys to extracting information for the Influence Map is to create High-Yield Questions, which we will discuss in detail in later chapters. High-Yield Questions produce the greatest amount of information in the shortest amount of time. As well, they are always structured in such a way that they appear to be for the benefit of the buyer as opposed to the benefit of the seller. Consider, for instance, the difference between these two questions:

o Who are the decision makers in this transaction?
o Let's make sure we have the appropriate resources lined up. Who are the people who need to be comfortable with the solution?

The first question appears self-serving; the latter—a High-Yield Question—tells the buyer you are trying to help.

As you advance through this process, you will likely uncover information about several people who will be influential in the decision-making process. Your plan needs to include how to earn the right to meet with those people you have not yet covered. Here are a few strategies that you might consider when developing your plan:

1. Leverage the contacts you currently have. Make sure you have a valid business reason for the introduction. Step into the shoes of the person you would like to meet and ask yourself what you would want a salesperson to do if you were the buyer.
2. Analyze the business issues for which they are most likely to want solutions.
3. Develop a list of their peers you have helped who might introduce you and validate your position as a helpful seller.
4. Consider contacts outside of their organization who might broker an introduction for you, giving you a different level of credibility.

When used with a Collaboration Map—which indentifies business issues, challenges, and consequences with business owners—Influence Maps allow sellers to identify with whom they should meet and what the subject of the meeting should be. While Collaboration Maps should be shared with the buyers, Influence Maps may contain sensitive or potentially offensive information about buyers and should not be shared. If Anna sees an Influence Map noting that you perceive Linda to be more influential, Anna may be offended, and her preference will be shifted away from you. However, with the proper risk assessment—ask yourself: *What is the worse thing that could happen?* and make a decision accordingly—an Influence Map could be shared with a Coach on the buying team. To minimize risk, collaborate with a potential Coach only on the portions of the Influence Map that are blank. As you become more and more comfortable with your Coach and you are sure of your relationship, you might disclose more, asking for help switching preference or identifying those who have influence.

CHAPTER 5

Competitive Maps

Understanding the Competitive Landscape

> "If you ain't first, you're last."
> —Ricky Bobby, NASCAR driver character in *Talladega Nights*

The idea that "perception is reality" as it relates to buyers keeps coming up. The impressions that a buyer develops about a seller, team, solution, and organization become the scorecard for choosing whether to do business with a particular seller or with someone else.

When thinking of competition, the first thing that typically comes to mind is sports. Thousands of coaches have talked about inspiration, teamwork, leadership, competition, and what it takes to be number one. The difference between first place and second place, they say, can be a hundredth of a second, the winner's breakfast, or a good night's sleep. On any given day, the smallest change could turn a winner into a second-placer, which is why coaches watch game tapes and study the competition to ensure they have an advantage on game day.

Let's look at golf.

In the 2009 PGA standings, the difference between first place and second place was only about one stroke. That's right: only about one stroke separated first and second place!

Standings as of April 2009

PLACE	GOLFER	AVG. SCORE
1	Geoff Ogilvy	69.43
2	Phil Mickelson	70.57
3	Kenny Perry	69.34
6	Zach Johnson	70.00
8	Brian Gay	69.56
11	Tiger Woods	69.33
26	David Toms	69.53
30	Jim Furyk	69.57
97	Jerry Kelly	69.83

These golfers are competitive; they never approach a round of golf hoping for a decent outcome. Each one of them wants to win. And, as often as they play golf, they still practice and practice, using coaches to look for ways to gain the competitive edge.

Looking at these scores you can see why a competitive edge in golf is so important. You will notice that a mere 1.24 strokes separates the highest and lowest average scores. Talk about a sport that requires some serious competitive planning and execution!

Now, let's look at how performance impacts earnings.

Standings as of April 2009

PLACE	GOLFER	AVG. SCORE	EARNINGS	EVENTS	EARNINGS PER EVENT
1	Geoff Ogilvy	69.43	$3,040,237	8	$380,029
2	Phil Mickelson	70.57	$3,004,290	8	$375,536
3	Kenny Perry	69.34	$2,612,263	10	$261,226
6	Zach Johnson	70.00	$1,850,080	10	$185,008
8	Brian Gay	69.56	$1,690,375	11	$153,670
11	Tiger Woods	69.33	$1,560,313	4	$390,038
26	David Toms	69.53	$925,505	8	$115,688
30	Jim Furyk	69.57	$862,581	8	$107,822
97	Jerry Kelly	69.83	$291,130	9	$32,347

The earnings difference between Geoff Ogilvy (first place) and Jerry Kelly (who placed ninety-seventh) is approximately $2.7 million. Only 0.4 stroke separates the first place from the ninety-seventh place, but the difference in rewards is huge.

Another interesting point is Kenny Perry, third-place winner, who earned about $430,000 less and had to play in two more events than Geoff Ogilvy. Perry obviously had to work harder, but he did not come in first. Considering average earnings per tournament, Ogilvy sits at $380,029 per event, Perry at $261,226 per event, and Jerry Kelly at $32,347 per event with a stroke difference of 0.49, less than one stroke.

I introduce this example to illustrate some of the key points that will be discussed in this chapter as well as the next one.

The first key point is that research, diligence, thorough planning, strong execution, and never settling for

the status quo keep a competitor sharp. Just like golf, small differences in your game have tremendous impact on your personal revenue as well as the revenue of your organization.

The second key point is that not all competitive battles can be won. Competitors choose the opportunities that they can win. Tiger Woods participated in only four events, but his average earnings were $390,038, slightly higher than Geoff Ogilvy's.

But unlike the game of golf, the game of sales has only one winner. No compensation is given for anything other than first place.

Assessing the Competitive Landscape

To assess your competitive position and come up with an effective strategy, you must start by thoroughly and objectively assessing your position and the position of the competitive alternatives. To be effective and provide clarity to the buying situation, you must remember to consider this assessment from the eye of the buyer so that you can see the same alternatives as the buyer.

This might sound simple, but how do you make sure you are paying attention to the buyer's perspective? How do you ensure that you come to the right conclusions?

I suggest using a Competitive Map, which is very simply a side-by-side analysis of why a buyer might choose your solution, a competitor's solution, or no solution at all.

Start by drawing a table with three columns: one column lists all the buyer's alternatives as far as a solution is concerned; one column assesses why the buyer would choose an alternative; and the third column assesses why the buyer would not choose an alternative.

As for rows, add as many as there are competitors. Let's say the buyer is considering your solution and two others. In addition to these two competitors, you need to consider if the buyer could do nothing or build the solution internally. In this case, you would have a table with three columns and four rows (in addition to the title row).

Your competitive assessment table will look something like this:

ALTERNATIVE	WHY WOULD THE BUYER CHOOSE?	WHY WOULDN'T THE BUYER CHOOSE?
Competitor 1		
Competitor 2		
Do Nothing/Build the Solution Internally		
My Solution		

You then want to consider, from the buyer's perspective, the answers to two questions, filling in the table appropriately.

○ Why would the buyer choose Competitor 1?
○ Why wouldn't the buyer choose Competitor 1?

Then move along to Competitor 2, asking the same questions before considering why the buyer might or might not choose to do nothing. Finally, ask yourself why the buyer would and would not choose your solution.

Putting yourself in the role of the buyer to come up with a strong and, insofar as it is possible, unbiased list of what the buyer likes about each solution gives you better insight into the buyer's thinking, which in turn allows you to determine the best strategy to win. It also helps you identify the competitive traps you might want to set so that the buyer shifts preference to your solution. (Competitive traps are covered at length in Chapter 8.)

Consider the relationship between Larry of Outstanding Options and Anna of Hargrove. Outstanding Options was competing against two formal competitors for the sales-effectiveness software solution that Hargrove was considering for its sales force. Larry used the following assessment to assist in determining his strategy to win. After completing this assessment, Larry came to the conclusion that Hargrove might choose Competitor 1, Front Line Selling Solutions. Let's take a look.

ALTERNATIVE	WHY WOULD HARGROVE CHOOSE . . . ?	WHY WOULDN'T HARGROVE CHOOSE . . . ?
Front Line Selling Solutions (FLSS)	○ FLSS is the incumbent. ○ Hargrove has invested millions of dollars with FLSS. ○ FLSS is deployed globally. ○ Upgrade fee is less than a new purchase fee and provides enhanced functionality and ease of use.	○ FLSS is not flexible and requires IT maintenance. ○ FLSS is not an integrated solution with lead management or contact management. ○ Sales training is not available through technology.
Solution Brokers	○ Technology was tried and well liked in Asia. ○ It is an updated approach to sales and sales management. ○ It is comprehensive. ○ It can stand alone, allowing flexibility for sales teams to enter and analyze data. ○ E-learning is available.	○ The software is clunky. ○ The software is not integrated with training. ○ The software solution has a limited user base because it is new to the market. ○ Solution Brokers has little experience with U.S.-based sales forces. ○ It is expensive as compared to the upgrade of FLSS. ○ FLSS is familiar and less work to install and use.

continued

ALTERNATIVE	WHY WOULD HARGROVE CHOOSE . . . ?	WHY WOULDN'T HARGROVE CHOOSE . . . ?
Build the solution internally	o The software would be customized exactly to Hargrove's needs.	o Building is expensive. o Building is slow. o Building requires sales expertise. o Building the solution internally seems excessive, given that Hargrove already has a solution.
Outstanding Options (My Solution)	o North America salespeople have experience with Outstanding Options sales methodology. o The software is comprehensive. o It is sales 2.0 compliant. o It aligns with the future technology platform. o E-learning is available and integrated within the software solution.	o Hargrove would have to change everything it does as related to sales force effectiveness. It would be a full-blown implementation as opposed to an upgrade inclusive of change management activities. o It is expensive as compared to the upgrade of FLSS. o Asia prefers Solution Brokers. o FLSS is familiar and less work to install and use.

As Larry analyzed each of the points in the Competitive Map, he put himself in the shoes of Hargrove. Pretending to be a member of Anna's buying team, he asked himself the following questions:

o *What is really wrong with the FLSS solution? We [at Hargrove] are using it today. We just haven't done the upgrade.*
o *Aren't all sales force automation solutions basically the same?*
o *How disruptive would it be to change the language and the process of this company?*

- How disruptive would it be to integrate FLSS with our customer relationship management system to take care of contact and lead management?
- Is the real issue that we are not disciplined about the process? Couldn't we simply strengthen our process internally and avoid this solution entirely?
- Is the real issue that we haven't done reinforcement or follow-up training with our teams to improve their execution?
- Is the real issue that our managers don't know how to use the system or the process?
- Why would we change software solutions if they are all similar? Do we really need to implement a relaunch and really execute on change management principles?

Review and Reassess

As the Outstanding Options team began reviewing the Competitive Map and analyzing the strengths and weaknesses of each competitor, they realized the Hargrove team would likely decide to stay with the incumbent, Front Line Sales Solutions. Therefore, Larry determined that the team was either missing information—perhaps the sales team had failed to uncover information in previous conversations that would explain Hargrove's decision to consider a shift away from FLSS—or that Outstanding Options was simply fulfilling Hargrove's evaluation matrix, allowing the buying team to tell its management that the team members had done their due diligence, performed a thorough investigation, and preferred FLSS.

The Outstanding Options team then discussed their Coach inside Hargrove. They relived the meetings Larry had with Pat, evaluating Pat's actions. Pat had not only collaborated with Larry on the Collaboration Map, but he had also used it with his team in his communications regarding the project. Pat had set up a meeting with the Outstanding Options executives and had collaborated with Larry on the agenda for the executive meeting. Pat had been telling Larry who the enemies were in the account, sharing barriers to entry, so Outstanding Options had been prepared at each meeting to defeat the "enemies" and overcome these barriers.

Larry and the team all agreed that they did have a Coach on the buying team: Pat.

What about Outstanding Options showing the Competitive Map to Pat?

"We can't do that," said Michelle, a novice seller new to the team.

"Sure we can," said Larry, who had already shown Pat the Collaboration Map. "After all, what is the worst thing that could possibly happen? We have already decided that if we were the buyer, we would stay with the incumbent. Based on our analysis, we are losing. Why not take this to Pat and see if we are missing any pertinent information? It's as simple as asking, 'Why are you interested in moving away from your current solution provider?'"

The Coach, Pat, listened carefully as Larry laid out the details of the Competitive Map. Pat was impressed that Outstanding Options had considered the eye of the buyer, looking at the solution through Hargrove's eyes.

Pat then went on to tell Larry something he did not know: FLSS had not really been used very well within Hargrove because the sales teams consider it administratively burdensome. In addition, Larry had been wrong about the upgrade fee for FLSS. Though one of the module's upgrade fee was significantly less than the Outstanding Options solution, Hargrove would have to upgrade all FLSS modules, making the price on par with the price of the Outstanding Options solution.

Pat also noted that Solution Brokers' Asian connection was not that important. Asia represented only 15 percent of Hargrove's revenue, whereas the United States represented 55 percent of Hargrove's revenue. And given Solution Brokers' lack of customer base and new entry to the software market, Pat assumed the deal would not go to Solution Brokers. In fact, Pat thought the competition was between FLSS and Outstanding Options.

This information drastically shifted Larry's assessment of the competitive landscape. In addition, Larry did some further due diligence on FLSS, updating the Competitive Map accordingly:

ALTERNATIVE	WHY WOULD HARGROVE CHOOSE . . . ?	WHY WOULDN'T HARGROVE CHOOSE . . . ?
Front Line Sales Solutions	o FLSS is the incumbent. o Hargrove has invested millions of dollars with FLSS. o It is deployed globally.	o FLSS is not flexible and requires IT maintenance. o FLSS is not an integrated solution with lead management or contact management. o Sales training is not available through technology. o The sales team considers FLSS administratively burdensome. o FLSS is not used well or consistently.

continued

ALTERNATIVE	WHY WOULD HARGROVE CHOOSE . . . ?	WHY WOULDN'T HARGROVE CHOOSE . . . ?
Solution Brokers	o Technology was tried and well liked in Asia. o It is an updated approach to sales and sales management. o It is comprehensive. o It can stand alone, allowing flexibility for sales teams to enter and analyze data. o E-learning is available.	o The software is clunky. o The software is not integrated with training. o The software solution has a limited user base because it is new to the market. o Solution Brokers has little experience with U.S.-based sales forces. o Asia represents only 15 percent of the revenues. Might not be a good fit for the rest of the world. o Solution Brokers is new to software solutions. o Very limited customer base in place today.
Build the solution internally	o The software would be customized exactly to Hargrove's needs.	o It is expensive. o It is slow. o It requires sales expertise. o Building the solution internally seems excessive, given that Hargrove already has a solution.
Outstanding Options (My Solution)	o North America salespeople have experience with Outstanding Options' sales methodology. o North America represents 55 percent of sales. o The software is comprehensive. o It is sales 2.0 compliant. o It aligns with the future technology platform. o E-learning is available and integrated within the software solution.	o FLSS is familiar and less work to install and use. o Hargrove would have to change everything it does as related to sales-force effectiveness. It would be a full-blown implementation as opposed to an upgrade inclusive of change-management activities.

And from this, Larry knew what he had to do to pick a winning strategy. He would choose a Flanking Strategy (discussed in the next chapter), changing the rules so the buyer was focusing on sales effectiveness and the seller's stability rather than the current focus: the time to transition to the new solution and the integration with global solutions.

Using Maps to Pick Your Strategy

When thinking of your strategy, you might jump into a description of all the activities you plan to perform. And while that description might make sense to people on the sales team, it is not a strategy in and of itself. The risk in using a list of activities to describe an overall strategy is that the approach may remain the same, even if the activities are different.

For instance, let's say you are trying to win two bids with two different buyers. For Buyer #1, you will demonstrate your solution, use customer testimonials, and invite the buyer to watch a customer using the solution in action. For Buyer #2, you will gather current costs, calculate ROI, present the analysis to executives, and show the superior savings.

Yes, the activities are different, but your approach is the same: Your approach is to show both buyers that you are better, stronger, and shinier than the competitors. Later in this chapter, you will learn that this is called a Frontal Strategy, and it might not be the correct strategy for Buyer #2. Without this guiding framework, though, you will be unable to sort through all available activities and select only those relevant to your strategy.

A true strategy provides the framework and guidance for the actions or activities you choose to deploy for developing preference over other solutions (including the solution of "do nothing"). In other words, it is an overarching umbrella that all activities must support. Using a military analogy, consider a Frontal Strategy. In this strategy, the army must be bigger, better, and stronger to win the battle. They might increase numbers and supply troops with the best weaponry; both activities are meant to support the strategy.

Compare this to Flanking, a strategy used by the American minutemen in the American Revolutionary War. They did not have the resources to be bigger, better, and stronger. Instead, they changed the rules. The Flanking Strategy meant that the minutemen would set new rules, discarding the traditional and formal lines and columns used in battles. Instead, by twisting the rules in their favor, they would go on to win the battles and the war. Some wore war paint reminiscent of Native Americans, relying on fear to intimidate the enemy. They used hunting rifles with long-range accuracy. Sharpshooters hid in trees to take out the enemy. The British troops marched in rigid lines, hoping to win by the old rules of a Frontal Strategy. Flanking changed these rules, and the activities the minutemen used to support their strategy proved to upset their enemies.

Selecting the right type of strategy requires that you have a wide and deep understanding of the situation, including:

1. The business challenge, which you learned from your Collaboration Map in Chapter 3.
2. The people who vote, which you learned from your Influence Map in Chapter 4.
3. The competitive assessment or the competitive landscape, which you learned from your Competitive Map when you evaluated the other solutions and alternatives in Chapter 5.

Without this information, your activities will be purely tactical rather than strategic. These activities can quickly degenerate into flailing and failing. If you do not know where you are going, then heed the words of the Cheshire Cat: "Any road will take you there."

A better approach, one that considers the end goal along with the reality of the situation, is to choose among four primary competitive strategies:

1. Frontal Strategy
2. Flanking Strategy
3. Fragment Strategy
4. Defend Strategy

Upon selecting a strategy, you can then choose activities that support this strategy, making sure that all demonstrations, white papers, ROIs, proposals, and messages to the buyer align with this strategy, as do the success stories you tell the buyer. Let's look at each strategy, as well as activities that support these strategies.

Frontal Strategy

Here, the goal is to tell the buyer that your solution is bigger, stronger, better, and more appropriate than the alternatives. This strategy is typically effective only if your solution is *obviously* better—hands-down, ultimately superior, no-questions-asked better than the next viable alternative. A Frontal Strategy is effective if:

o You have a solution that no one else has
o You have a window of general availability that is unique
o You have some secret sauce that makes your solution extremely superior

If you choose a Frontal Strategy, you might

o Lead meetings with solution demonstrations that show your obvious superiority
o Explain that your solution dominates the market and holds the spot as the industry leader
o Showcase your astounding and impressive roster of happy customers

The Frontal Strategy is seen everywhere. Pepsi's "Pepsi Challenge" relied on the Frontal Strategy to promote Pepsi in blind taste tests with its largest competitor, Coca-Cola. Miller Lite's "Great taste . . . less filling" campaign is a Frontal Strategy. In fact, this is the most often chosen strategy. It does not, however, often translate to the most winning strategy. A Frontal Strategy is appropriate only if 99 percent of people would choose your solution in a head-to-head comparison. Otherwise, you should choose another strategy.

Flanking Strategy

Flanking is appropriate if you know that your solution is not the obvious winner in a head-to-head comparison. Flanking allows you to change the rules so that the solutions are evaluated based on some aspect in which you are the leader. Using our military analogy, consider that the Taliban changed the rules by using suicide bombers. When the Scots, as portrayed in the movie *Braveheart*, were confronted by the British, the Scots were clearly outnumbered and out-armed, which meant they had to change the rules.

In business, you might rely on a Flanking Strategy if you want your buyer to focus on your customer service because the solutions all look the same. You would then compete not on solution ability but rather on the strength of your customer service team. All cable companies might look the same, but one that bundles high-speed Internet access, cable, and phone service can use a Flanking Strategy to beat its competitors.

If you have a solution that radically changes the game or uses a completely different approach from what is traditionally available, then it is to your advantage to change the rules for how buyers evaluate.

Keep in mind that the strategy guides the actions. The biggest mistake salespeople make when choosing a Flanking Strategy is to use Frontal Strategy activities to support the strategy. For instance, I recently met with a client who wanted to discuss her strategy for winning a certain buyer. She walked me through her Collaboration, Influence, and Competitive Maps. Clearly, all the competitive solutions were similar.

"Which of the four strategies are you considering?" I asked.

"All the solutions look the same in the eye of the buyer, so Frontal will not work. I need to change the rules to create a competitive advantage. I think I should flank the competition."

I agreed. Then I asked, "What activities are you planning to support this activity?"

"I am going to use the ROI with the buyer," she said.

"Great. What will your competition use?" I asked.

A light turned on for my client. "They will probably use the ROI as well."

Given that the competition would be using the same tool, her ROI supported a Frontal Strategy. The ROI would result in a head-to-head comparison. To truly use a Flanking Strategy, she needed to use something that her competition would not be using. Together, we came up with a plan: We would provide the buyer with a risk assessment that enabled the buying team to better plan for successful implementation—eliminate all the typical surprises that delay projects of this sort and drive costs up. My client knew that none of her competitors could offer a risk assessment for free. She would change the rules from product evaluation to a reduction of implementation-related risk, thereby saving the client time and adding value to the solution.

Back to Larry's dilemma, Larry knew that Hargrove had been focused on the amount of time it would take to transition to a new solution. FLSS perhaps wasn't the superior solution, but it was used at Hargrove and was the global solution of choice. Transitioning to a new software would cost Hargrove considerable time.

Larry decided to move the focus away from this. Instead, he would focus on sales effectiveness and the stability of his company. In doing this, he would remove the focus from the weaknesses of Outstanding Options and place the focus on its strengths.

Fragment Strategy

Sometimes you must acknowledge that you cannot win the entire deal, but you might win a piece of the deal. A Fragment Strategy allows you to establish a niche and win a piece of the business by getting the buyers to focus on the pieces you do best.

In a Fragment Strategy, your goal is to convince the buyers to choose certain components from you and others from other providers or alternatives. Let's consider stroller shopping, the bane of any new parent's shopping excursions. Strollers come in all sizes and shapes. Suppose the highest-functioning stroller is likely so heavy that it will break the new mother's back if she tries to load the stroller into the trunk of her car. A lightweight stroller has little room for storage; it also is bumpy and has few (if any) amenities. Sure, that new mom can easily lift it off the ground, but she'll be carrying the diaper bag and her bottle of water since the stroller offers no storage.

Enter car seats, some of which are sold with strollers as a set, whereas others are sold alone. The best-functioning, highest-rated car seat might not fit with the best stroller. But a car seat manufacturer with a less-than-ideal stroller should choose a fragmented approach to win business if its car seat is rated best in safety. Every new parent on the block would want to make sure that his or her baby is fully protected in the event of a car accident!

Those who choose a Fragment Strategy convince the buyers to choose the best pieces of each solution, putting them together for a great overall solution. In other words, the seller gets the buyer focused on the piece of business where the seller is the strongest. Once that piece of business is secure, the seller has a foot in the door and can work to expand business with the buyer.

Defend Strategy

In this strategy, the seller is the incumbent and wants to leverage his or her position as the current provider and keep competitors out. You should use this strategy to protect existing accounts and your positions within those accounts. This strategy usually includes more proactive activities with your existing customers, such as conducting regular executive/business briefings; establishing and maintaining good, strong communication with the customer; and making sure that the customer constantly understands the business value of the relationship.

Like all strategies, the Defend Strategy must be supported using specific tactics. I recently coached a sales team on a presentation to be delivered by three sales team members. The sales team wanted to do a dry run of the presentation to work out any kinks before they presented in front of the buyer. Before they started their presentation, they told me they planned to use the Defend Strategy because the buyer was an existing customer with whom the seller had a strong relationship.

The team went on to deliver a presentation that focused on the buyer's current business challenge, explaining how the seller's solution would benefit the buyer.

"How is this different from the strategy your competitors will use?" I asked, knowing the answer.

Again, the actions were geared toward a Frontal Strategy and did not support a Defend Strategy. We reworked their presentation to focus on elements of their established customer relationship:

o The key successes they had with the buyer, reminding the buyer that the solution would continue to offer these sorts of benefits
o The relationships with buying executives who support the sellers and the business results they have been able to achieve
o The fact that they were always on time and under budget with all previous projects

Tactical Overlays

In the world of selling, most people call activities that support strategies "strategy overlays." I call them "tactical overlays" because they are not strategies, but rather activities to support one of the four strategies outlined in this chapter.

Remember that all tactics/activities must be tied to a strategy. Here, we will discuss some of these activities, as well as the corresponding strategies they might support.

○ **Preempt.** A successful preemptive overlay blocks the competition from participating in the evaluation or working with the buyer. If your buyer is a current customer who is happy, this tactic is appropriate when used in conjunction with a defensive strategy. It can also be used with a Frontal Strategy if your solution is so obviously superior that the buyer would agree to an exclusive. For instance, if an existing customer is considering additional solution capabilities, you could leverage the relationship by telling the buyer that time and money can be saved by considering your solution first. If it is not a good fit, then the customer can open the evaluation to other solutions.

○ **Affect timing.** A timing overlay either delays or accelerates the process. The timing tactics allow you to accelerate or slow down a deal depending on your overall strategy. Timing tactics will support any of the four primary strategies. For example, if your solution is superior, you can overlay a frontal strategy with a timing acceleration, which allows you to speed up the deal before your competition can develop a Flanking Strategy to change the rules. On the other hand, if your solution is not superior, you can combat a Frontal Strategy by delaying the timing to allow you to create an effective Flanking Strategy.

A classic speed-up strategy would be to offer a discount to buyers who make decisions by a certain date. A slowdown tactic might be to conduct a pilot, which would cause the buyer to look more deeply at your solution with the intention of growing your superiority in key functional areas.

○ **Walk away/pull away.** You might be shocked to hear this, but sometimes you should simply walk away from a deal. When the rules are not giving you a fair opportunity to compete, you should simply decline the opportunity. This is, in fact, a tactic that is part of an overall strategy: If you walk away or pull away from a deal, you are changing the rules as part of a Flanking Strategy.

KNOWING IS NOT THE SAME AS DOING

When you pull away, you might say, "We have elected to withdraw from the evaluation process as we are concerned that we may not be a good fit based on the limited access we have had with your organization. We want to be considerate of your time and resources."

If the buyer does not call you back, you were likely going to lose anyway, so you just saved yourself time and resources. If the buyer calls you back, then you have an opportunity to change the rules or execute your Flanking Strategy, perhaps by asking for executive access to clarify the business metrics that would define success of an implemented solution.

The Formula for Selecting a Strategy

The most common mistake salespeople make is selecting a strategy before they have sufficient information. Another common mistake is failing to specifically connect their actions and messages to the selected strategy. The formula for selecting a strategy is to:

1. Understand the buyer's business challenges
2. Understand the people
3. Understand the competitive landscape

Armed with this information, salespeople can analyze which strategy to execute in order to win. Next, using their knowledge of the buyer's business challenges, people, and competitive landscape, they can align the following to support their chosen strategy:

- Activities
- Messages
- Success stories
- Relationships
- Behaviors
- Tools
- Value statements

PART 3

IMPLEMENTING STRATEGY

Upon selecting a strategy, the selling and buying process becomes a little less straightforward. The seller's goal is to continue taking actions that allow the process to advance. Herein, we discuss a variety of tools and methodologies that allow this to occur:

○ A Joint Evaluation Plan, the subject of Chapter 7, creates milestones upon which both the buyer and seller agree, establishing opportunities for the seller to advance.

○ In Chapter 8, you, the seller, learn to be intentional about the language and vocabulary you use when establishing your competitive advantage, setting Competitive Traps, and responding to Competitive Traps.

○ How taking the time to formulate High-Yield Questions can set the stage for the buyer to advance is the subject of Chapter 9.

○ In the next two chapters, I'll discuss how to put all your isolated tools together for not only an effective meeting (Chapter 10, "Your Call Plan") but also a winning sales process (Chapter 11, "The Overview: Your Customer Game Plan").

○ In the final chapter, Chapter 12, "Delivery," we discuss establishing a buyer-centric culture. A buyer-centric culture is a true paradigm shift in the world of sales and one that will create long-term competitive advantage.

CHAPTER 7

The Joint Evaluation Plan

> "Plan your work for today and every day, then work your plan."
> —Norman Vincent Peale, Christian preacher and author of
> *The Power of Positive Thinking*

By this stage in the game, you are ready to start implementing your plan for working with the buying team. We look to the Joint Evaluation Plan (JEP) that allows you to collaborate with your buyer in analyzing your solution and its efficacy in meeting the buyer's goals. The Joint Evaluation Plan is a collaborative tool meant to be used with the buyer. It accomplishes the following:

o Sets expectations
o Maps the course to the end

- Establishes the resources that need to be available to come to a decision
- Provides for measurement of the buyer and seller's progress as they work together to come to a conclusion
- Reflects the suggested actions you need to support your strategy and keep the sales team and buying team on the same page

Remember that a buyer who is evaluating your solution also has a full-time job. Evaluating your solution is likely a project that is added to the buyer's normal workloads. Just like you, the buyer would like to come to a positive decision in the shortest period of time so it can get back to the job at hand. A Joint Evaluation Plan helps the buyer move more quickly, which means you are providing a tremendous amount in helping the buyer take on this extra workload of evaluating solutions. In other words, a JEP allows the buyer to see the course instead of fumbling in the dark.

As well, the Joint Evaluation Plan is a great test the seller can use to determine

- Whether a Coach has been located
- Whether the buyer has established preference
- The buyer's willingness to engage
- The buyer's level of seriousness about making a decision

To a great degree, the Joint Evaluation Plan can be summarized as a timeline that identifies several things for both the buyer and the seller, such as the steps; the go/no-go milestones; the start and end dates; and the resources, events, and objectives of both buyer and seller. The Joint Evaluation Plan gives both the buyer and the seller an advantage.

Value of a Joint Evaluation Plan

SELLER'S ADVANTAGES	BUYER'S ADVANTAGES
Pinpoints the activities for which the buyer needs to come to a conclusion.	Sets clear expectations on the activities necessary for the buyer to properly evaluate a solution.
Plans for the resources that will be needed to fulfill the buyer's requirements.	Outlines the resources the buyer expects from the seller.
Measures where the seller is in the sales process versus where the buyer is in the buying process.	Sets clear expectations on dates to be adhered to in the schedule.
Communicates to the buying team in a nonmanipulative way when the evaluation has fallen behind schedule or when the buyers have not held up their end of the bargain.	Identifies when the sellers are not holding up their end of the bargain.
Identifies the points of risk or disconnects along the way so that they can be addressed immediately.	Puts all the sellers on the same schedule, providing a fair evaluation process.

The Joint Evaluation Plan doesn't have to be elaborate; it just has to be clear. A basic letter of understanding about the events, activities, and resources that were previously agreed to, as well as when they are expected and which party is responsible for delivering them, constitutes a Joint Evaluation Plan.

As long as it is prepared jointly, the JEP can be changed. For example:

Joint Evaluation Plan					Decision Date _____

Tasks/Activities/Events	Objective	Responsible	By When	Status
Understand Business Challenge				
Continue? Yes/No				
Collaborate on Possible Solution				
Continue? Yes/No				
Validate Solution				
Continue? Yes/No				
Collaborate on Proposal				
Continue? Yes/No				
Accept Proposal				
Special Notes:				

The Joint Evaluation Plan lets the buyer know that both the buyer and the seller are engaged in the same process, and both are responsible for determining how they will work together. When done collaboratively, it creates a psychological bridge between seller and buyer, putting them on the same team.

It also creates a visual alignment of the selling and buying processes with verifiable outcomes to show how the seller can continue to consider the eye of the buyer, while the buyer remains engaged and aware of the process. It avoids the normal recipe for failure: having the sales team inform the buyer as to how the sales process will proceed.

Consider Larry and Anna's meeting for an example of how a JEP can establish a positive relationship between buyer and seller.

Hargrove had been a longtime customer of Outstanding Options. However, Larry was a new sales rep for Outstanding Options. He was completely unknown to Anna, his point of contact at Hargrove. The previous sales rep had done an outstanding job of making Anna angry, especially at month- or quarter-end when the previous sales rep needed to push a deal to close. Although Anna has had this experience with many sales reps over the years, her patience had run thin.

When Larry introduced himself for the first time, Anna was exasperated. Yet again, she has a new rep to educate. She agreed to meet with Larry to set the record straight.

Upon the first meeting, Anna let Larry have it: all of her frustrations with previous tactics and pressure to close business on the seller's schedule were unloaded on Larry. Larry was gracious. He appreciated the pain Anna had suffered because he certainly would have felt the same way. However, he was confident he had a solution to assist Hargrove in building a positive relationship. You see, Larry was an avid fan of the Joint Evaluation Plan. Larry knew that securing Anna's business would help benefit his quota assignment; he also knew the relationship needed to be in place before he could gain that business.

After Anna unloaded, Larry suggested that they work together to define the timeline and expectations on this next evaluation so that he would not make the same mistakes as his predecessor. Anna liked this idea.

"For the first time, I felt like I might have some control over the process," she later told us.

Together, Larry and Anna sketched a plan, setting start and end dates, as well as milestones and decision points. Anna pinpointed the activities and resources she needed to properly evaluate, making commitments as to what she would provide to help Larry deliver these resources.

Larry promptly went back to his office and put this conversation into a Joint Evaluation Plan, e-mailing the file to Anna with a note asking her to confirm that he had understood their conversation.

"I was thrilled with what I had in front of me. I felt like my time would be honored and that the solution was truly going to be one that I felt confident about, should we select it," she said of the initial interaction with Larry.

As the evaluation progressed, Anna's busy schedule put them further and further behind in their target dates. Larry was concerned; he was holding up his end of the bargain, but Anna was falling behind. This schedule slip would negatively impact Larry's forecast; however, he knew the relationship with Anna was a critical part of securing the business.

Fortunately, Larry had the Joint Evaluation Plan, which he was able to use to track all activities and resources in comparison to target dates. Clearly, Larry had held up his end of the bargain and needed to meet with Anna to get things back on track.

Anna was happy to grant the meeting to discuss progress against the plan. After all, she embraced the plan as her own. When they met to review the milestones and progress, Larry did not need to say anything about Anna's tardiness. It was abundantly clear that Larry had invested a tremendous amount of time and energy for Anna's benefit, yet Anna had not delivered on her end of the bargain.

Anna considered her behavior unacceptable as she had developed the plan and agreed to the terms of the plan. Instead of being angry with Outstanding Options, as she had been when she first met with Larry, Anna now felt that she had to clear up her reputation by delivering on her promises.

Anna immediately apologized to Larry, recognizing the level of effort Larry had put into building the relationship. She assured Larry that they would be on time with the decision, and she asked that she and Larry speak weekly to ensure all steps were being taken to close the deal.

In doing this, Anna gave Larry a competitive edge. He was building a solid relationship with Anna.

Later, Anna revealed something. She suspected the previous sales rep was going through the same effort and that she had always held up progress. Likely, the previous sales rep had also put pressure on Anna to move forward, but because the two had not created a Joint Evaluation Plan, Anna had lost perspective on the time and effort he expended on her behalf.

The "pressure" the previous sales rep then placed on Anna to make a decision seemed unreasonable to Anna, which meant the relationship was forever damaged. When Larry replaced this sales representative and introduced the Joint Evaluation Plan, Anna could see, in black and white, that she had not fulfilled her obligations. Rather than feeling pressured, she jumped into action by moving heaven and earth to make sure she delivered on her commitments.

Initially, you may find that a buyer is hesitant and skeptical about the Joint Evaluation Plan. Buyers are cautious of

Joint Evaluation Plan

Decision Date _____

Go-Live Date _____

Tasks/Activities/Events	Objective	Responsible	By When	Status
Understand Business Challenge				
Meeting with All Recommenders		*Larry/Anna*	*Dec*	*Dec*
Continue? Yes/No *Business Case Confirmed*				
Collaborate on Possible Solution				
Solution Work Session		*Larry/Anna*	*Jan*	*Jan*
Continue? Yes/No				
Validate Solution				
Solution Presentation w/ Decision Makers		*Larry*	*Feb*	*Feb*
Continue? Yes/No *Solution Confirmed*				
Collaborate on Proposal				
Proposal Work Session		*Anna*	*March*	*March*
Continue? Yes/No *Proposal Submitted*				
Accept Proposal				
Attorney Involvement			*Apr/May*	*Apr/May*
Special Notes: *Reach Agreement*				

manipulative sales teams because they want to be in control of their buying process. For that reason, clearly articulating the value that a Joint Evaluation Plan brings to the buyer is critical. Creating a JEP is considerate as it takes some of the work off the buyer's plate while still allowing the buyer to shape the process. The plan communicates to the buyer that the seller wants to have all resources available to the buyer so as not to delay the decision process, thereby allowing the buyer to get on with his or her real job.

The first step in the Joint Evaluation Plan is to identify the steps that the buyer and seller will expect from the process. Again, use examples to help the buyer become comfortable with this process. Using our example of the buying process, let's see what tasks the buyer might identify when trying to evaluate and validate this point in the process:

o "Review all Requests for Proposals (RFPs) to gain a short list of vendors to review by February 1."
o "Allow each vendor to meet with the team to understand our challenges and what we are trying to accomplish with a new solution."
o "Listen to each proposal presentation and select a short list to recommend to management."
o "Present recommendation to management."
o "Gain approval from management and negotiate the contract."
o "Begin implementation by April 1."

Using our experience as sellers, we may want to insert some suggested activities to help the buyer come to a decision:

o "Offer a template RFP that the buyer can change or modify according to needs, enabling the buyer to speed up the grueling task of writing an RFP."
o "Allow scheduled phone discussions with sellers in the event they need to clarify understanding of the RFP and the priority of the questions."
o "Review all RFPs to gain a short list of vendors to review by February 1."
o "Allow each vendor to meet with the team to understand the buyer's challenges and what we are trying to accomplish with a new solution."
o "Allow visits and conference calls to collaborate with the buyer on a possible solution."

○ "Define the criteria for selection so the sellers will focus on the buyer's priorities."

○ "Listen to each proposal presentation and select a short list to recommend to management."

○ "Select short-listed sellers to assist with any presentation materials that may be needed for management presentation."

○ "Begin understanding of what will be necessary in negotiation or contract process so sellers are prepared, eliminating any potential barriers for buyers."

○ "Present recommendation to management."

○ "Gain approval from management and negotiate the contract."

○ "Begin implementation by April 1."

By creating a Joint Evaluation Plan, the seller is immediately collaborating with the buyer, working as a team on small activities that begin to establish collaboration, as well as setting the expectation of a future collaboration. The seller is helping the buyer eliminate any future surprises or barriers and is trying to make the process easier as part of the up-front planning exercises. Clarifying intent and expectations early on leads to a much more productive selling and buying experience while avoiding late-stage bottlenecks and delays in the evaluation process.

CHAPTER 8

Positioning Your Message to Support the Strategy

> "The success of the strategy rests in people's execution."
> —Dennis Donovan, Former Executive Vice President of
> Human Resources for Home Depot, Inc.

W hen it comes to communicating with your buyer, you might think the best course of action is to simply respond instinctively. But like the entire sales process, communicating with the buyer requires forethought. Herein, we consider two elements of communicating with the buyer:

1. Communicating competitive advantages.
2. Dealing with competitive traps.

In fact, these two components are not all that different. By learning to deal effectively with competitive traps, you might succeed in communicating a competitive advantage and establish preference for your solution.

Competitive Advantages

One thing is sure: if you don't articulate the value that your solution brings over alternatives, no one will articulate this value on your behalf. Conveying this value in a way that supports your strategy—in other words, communicating your competitive advantage—is critical to your ability to win a deal.

Almost always, though, sellers default to the Frontal Strategy when articulating this competitive position. They simply insist that their solution is better, stronger, or faster—even if it isn't. My theory on why the Frontal Strategy has become the default strategy is that most sellers analogize their process to competitive sports, whereby the better, stronger, and faster athletes are the ones who come out on top.

Or so we think.

Let's analyze why Tiger Woods wins in golf, or why Rafael Nadal wins in tennis. Is it because Woods and Nadal are better, faster, and stronger? Not necessarily, but Woods and Nadal both choose a strategy intentionally, and then they execute the strategy. The two men do not simply practice, practice, practice. They also strategize, try to match wits, and outperform their competition not only on skill but also on positioning.

Competitive positioning aligns your strategy with the message you deliver to your buyers. If you choose a Flanking Strategy, you must position your statements so that you change the rules that establish the framework your buyers will use to evaluate your product. If you choose a Defend Strategy, you must set the framework so that your buyers focus on why the solution is already working and how changing courses might upset the company's rhythm.

Aligning your competitive position with your strategy is not all that hard—assuming you spend time thinking about it. By positioning your message to support your strategy, you create a situation wherein you can communicate your differentiators early and often and find those that "stick." This allows your buyer to determine which solution is a better fit; at the same time, you are tilting the competition in your favor by setting the bar for all other alternatives, particularly if the seller is the first to present a competitive position.

If you let your buyer know early in the process why your solution has unique value, any competitor who may later articulate the same competitive advantage is seen as a copycat. Most often, a buyer will not explicitly communicate that another seller has beat the competitor to the punch, so your solution will have an advantage with the buyer.

Critical to setting the bar for competitive advantages is to collaborate with the buyer to make sure that you are communicating something new. When communicating with buyers about competitive advantages, the seller must have earned the right to ask the Coach whether the buying team has seen any similar competitive advantage in other solutions the team might be evaluating. If the Coach has not seen the advantage, the seller has set the bar for other alternatives. If the Coach has seen similar benefits in other solutions, the seller can look for other competitive advantages that are new and fresh, setting the bar for competitors who have not communicated these benefits.

Activity

Think of a current opportunity you are working on. List five reasons a buyer should select your solution over your competitor's:

1. _____
2. _____
3. _____
4. _____
5. _____

Now put yourself in the shoes of the buyer and evaluate this list. For each advantage, answer the following questions: Can your competitors say they have the same advantages as you? If not, then why aren't they the same? If so, what would you replace your competitive advantage with? In the space provided below, clarify how you would articulate your competitive message to address these questions.

1. _____
2. _____
3. _____
4. _____
5. _____

Too often, sellers overlook the benefits of communicating competitive advantages, avoiding any direct conversation with the buyers about their solution's differentiators. Most salespeople are concerned about their ability to effectively articulate their competitive positioning statements. Competitive advantage statements said with the wrong vocabulary can come across as arrogant, negative, offensive, dirty, ugly, sleazy, and unfair. If a seller comes across as too passionately opposed to the competition, the buyers might consider the seller to be engaging in unethical negative selling and take their business elsewhere.

Nonetheless, you do have to communicate your solution's advantages or the buyer will not know what they are. In other words, you have to do it, but you have to do it professionally, effectively, and nonoffensively.

In this chapter, we will show you how this is done.

Highlighting Your Strengths

When considering your competitive advantages, think about how to communicate your own strengths and not your competitor's weaknesses. In fact, you never want to articulate a competitor's weakness to a buyer. Doing so will backfire for several reasons:

1. You do not work for the competitor, so you cannot know the competitor's weaknesses.
2. Your buyers will consider this trash talk, which they consider playing dirty.
3. If you are wrong, your buyer might think you are lying or exaggerating, and this will call into question everything you have told the buyer in the past as well as everything you will tell the buyer in the future.

When it comes to your own solution, however, you clearly understand the advantages and strengths. In fact, knowing your strengths and weaknesses, and communicating these effectively, are the same as understanding your competitor's weaknesses. The difference is in how you communicate your advantages. By speaking only of your own company's strengths, you create the right impressions in the buyer's mind:

1. You do work for your company, so you should know all about its strengths.
2. When speaking positively of your solution, you sound enthusiastic instead of negative and unfair.
3. Rather than wasting your time gossiping about your competitor's weaknesses, you are concentrating on how your solution can align with the buyer's needs for the buyer's benefit.

In other words, you create an entirely different impression of how your company does business. Let's outline how Larry was able to maintain his creditability and professionalism when articulating Outstanding Options' competitive advantages by using a competitive message that focuses on the company's strengths.

As Larry and the sales team discussed the sales strategy, they thought about their main competitor, Front Line Sales Solutions, the solution Hargrove had been using for years.

Behind closed doors, Larry said this to his team:

FLSS does not provide a true sales effectiveness solution. Their solution still allows for the sales teams to put in unchecked data, and there are no training options integrated into the solution. The sales team actions are not checked against any methodology to help them sell. Sure, the reps input data, and it is reported on until the cows come home, but managers still have to spend time with manual inspection of the data to see if the sales teams are being realistic in their assessments, and sales reps still have to spend that time defending their position, and they still have to go off site for days of training. Where is the effectiveness in this?

MAKE IT PERSONAL

But when he met with Anna at Hargrove, Larry's message focused not on FLSS's weaknesses, but rather on Outstanding Options' strengths. Instead of bashing FLSS, he said:

Our customers have told us that we are the only alternative who can provide an integrated sales methodology. They say that our solution allows validation at the point of origin for the sales team. They have told us that our unique design makes integration instantaneous. Our customers say this validation at the point of origin allows the sales team to proactively change their strategy to win and allows the managers time to coach to win instead of having to inspect and train sales teams.

If he had bashed FLSS, Larry would have taken several unnecessary risks: First, he could have been wrong about FLSS's weaknesses, which would make him seem dishonest. Perhaps FLSS recently integrated its solution. Remember, too, that he might be talking to the FLSS Coach on the buying team, which means any "bashing" of FLSS would seem offensive and arrogant.

Instead, Larry focused on stating the positives about his solution. He communicated the same advantages, but in a far more positive and effective manner that maintained his integrity while connecting the solution to Hargrove's need to save cost and time. Consider what Anna might be thinking (as indicated below in parentheses) as Larry communicates his message in a positive and professional manner:

"Our customers have told us . . ." (This isn't Larry's opinion; this is his customers' opinion. Larry's customers must really like Outstanding

Options. That's comforting. And Larry seems humble. What a refreshing treat to work with a seller who isn't focused only on himself.)

"... *that we are the only alternative who can provide an integrated sales methodology. Our solution allows validation at the point of origin for the sales team.*" (That would be nice. We certainly don't have this with FLSS!)

"*They have told us that our unique design makes integration instantaneous.*" (Instantaneous integration surely would be a nice change!) "*Our customers say this validation at the point of origin allows the sales team to proactively change their strategy to win and allows the managers time to coach to win instead of having to inspect and train sales teams.*" (Interesting. Maybe the fact that the solution is more expensive isn't such a bad thing. After all, the transition would be a lot smoother.)

Clearly, focusing on your strengths rather than your competitor's weaknesses is more effective. Of course, to truly have an impact, it must be verifiable because the buyer is going to follow up to make sure that your strengths are indeed unique.

Managing Your Message

The strengths your solution brings to the table might be abundantly clear to you, but they will not be clear to a buyer unless you specifically articulate them. As the expert on your solution, you must educate the buyer about how your solution is unique and how these differentiators will impact the buyer's business. However, you must make the information manageable.

If you have hundreds of advantages, the buyer cannot remember, much less understand, all of them. Try to remember the first day you were employed by your current employer and that feeling of being overwhelmed as you learned about the offerings you would be selling. That overwhelmed feeling is the same feeling your buyer has when looking at your solutions. It is compounded because the buyer is not only considering your solution but also your competitors' solutions. The buyer must retain a great deal of information in a short period of time.

By managing your message, you will also keep it relevant. Remember to always communicate based on the eye of the buyer. Choose which differentiators you communicate based on the variables that matter to the buyer and the buyer's business as opposed to what you may think is sexy and cool. Provide examples the buyer can easily understand that will illustrate why your strong points are imperative to their success.

As well, keep the buyer's focus broad. Buyers tend to focus on details, trying to understand the features, functions, and mechanisms of a solution. Remember to keep the buyer connected to the overall big picture—the business value of your competitive advantage.

Aligning Your Strengths with Your Buyers' Needs

Buyers can retain only so much information, so out of the list of all differentiators, only those that are relevant should be revealed. If you have a Flanking Strategy, you might focus on the services that your company offers. But first you must determine whether the buyer cares about these services. Does your Collaboration Map give you any indication that the services your company offers have an impact on their ability to execute? What is your position in the marketplace?

As you consider all possible competitive advantages, the filter starts to look something like this:

1. All possible competitive advantages
2. Only those that address typical pains and issues in the industry
3. Only those that are relevant to the competitors in this opportunity
4. Only those relevant to the competitive strategy
5. Only those that represent actual pains and key business requirements relevant to this opportunity
6. Only those relevant to the key influencers in this opportunity

You will notice that the filter gets more specific as you learn more about a specific opportunity. On a first or an early call, the competitive messages you discuss might be based simply on your experience in the industry, but as you learn more about the business opportunity, you will begin to see which ones resonate with the buyer. Your competitive strategy and tactics will change based upon the competitive alternatives the buyer is considering. Eventually, you will

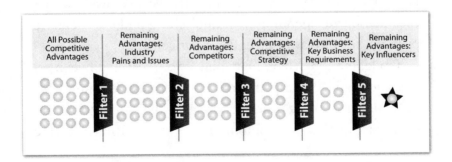

align your competitive messages with the buyer's Collaboration and Influence Maps.

Aligning Competitive Positioning to Mapping

We just talked about the filtering process in general, so how do you do that in a time-sensitive manner? You have already produced the key tools that will give you the bulk of the insight that you need for message alignment—the Collaboration Map and the Influence Map.

Let's talk first about the Collaboration Map. At the bottom layer of the Collaboration Map, you will find Tactical Pains that you have uncovered. Tactical Pains are the ones that can typically be solved with a product or solution.

If Hargrove suffers from the Tactical Pain of "invalidated data" in its sales effectiveness software, Larry might demonstrate how his solution would validate data entered based on a sales methodology.

To attach Larry's solution to Hargrove's needs, he will connect the dots so that he can show Anna the consequences of not solving these pains. He would ask questions that would lead Anna to uncover some knowledge: for example, the current sales-force automation software is too cumbersome for sales representatives to use, which means that sales teams are frustrated with Hargrove's administrative overhead, which means they are spending less time selling and are therefore putting the company's revenue in danger.

Collaboration Maps help make your competitive messages relevant to the pains and key business requirements. Let's look at another example. Imagine that you work for an organization that sells automation and reporting software for handling new employee applications, résumés, recruiting, and staffing. You recently had a conversation with Sean, manager of recruiting, and Maggie, the IT manager. Let's use the following Tactical Pains that you uncovered during a recent conversation to see how you would identify competitive points.

Sean shares with you that external applicants are highly frustrated with the amount of time and effort required to submit an application. Sean mentions that the company is losing candidates before they ever get them in the door. This is significant, as the lack of employees is affecting customer

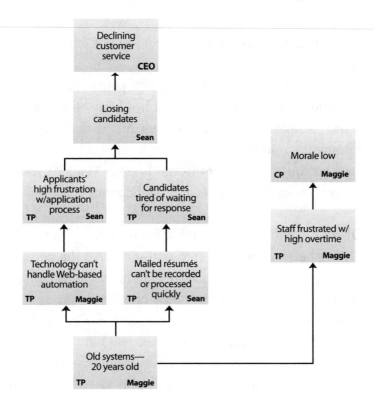

service. In addition, mail-in résumés cannot be recorded and processed quickly enough, so many candidates get tired of waiting to hear back, and they pursue other opportunities.

Maggie shared with you that the IT gets most of the blame for these inefficiencies—and rightfully so. She is working with systems that have been in place for twenty years, and these systems are not equipped to handle Web-based automation or the volume of paper résumés the company receives. Her staff is highly frustrated from working so much overtime.

Based upon this information, you want to share four key points with Sean and Maggie:

1. You offer a Web-based application process, known as Apply Now.
2. Your technology automatically scans paper résumés and consolidates résumé information from any other source.
3. Your technology platform takes advantage of the latest in automation and is extremely easy to maintain.
4. Your outsourcing services would free up Maggie's staff to focus on other IT projects and applications.

Of course, you are also working from a Competitive Map, which has better allowed you to consider what the competition is going to do. As you attach solutions to your Collaboration Map, you start to create a competitive scorecard that lets you know how you stack up against the competition. For each of your solution components, you have determined whether the competition is stronger, weaker, equal to you, or unknown. The bottom row of your map would look something like the following:

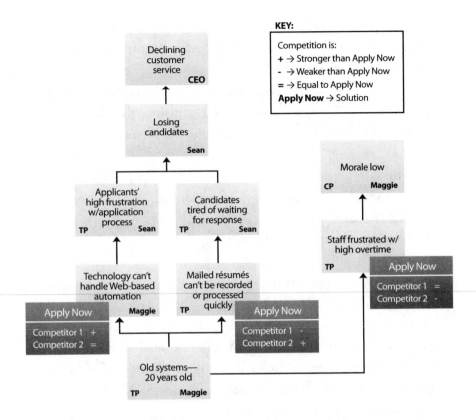

The second point of alignment is the Influence Map. Typically, on your Collaboration Map, each issue has an "owner." In this example, the key owners of these issues are Maggie and Sean. You should also review your Influence Map to see Maggie and Sean's levels of influence and their relationships to others who are influential. All owners should also be reflected on your Influence Map. In more complex sales situations, you might have dozens of Tactical Pains, and aligning competitive messages for all of them might not be possible or practical. To get the most bang for your buck, the points that you will want to concentrate on are those pains that are owned or tied directly to the people of influence.

Competitive messages always sound good in your head, but botching the delivery is all too easy. Remember: a fine line exists between effective and offensive when delivering competitive messages. To maintain your credibility, and for your message to sound professional, consider the three-part formula for articulating your message to a buyer:

1. The safety net
2. The specific differentiator or element of your solution that makes it a competitive advantage
3. Your declaration or indicator flag

Safety Net The competitive advantage sentence should begin with a safety net that softens what might be otherwise an absolute statement. An absolute statement can sound arrogant, boastful, or self-serving. A seller's objective is to guide the buyer to come to prefer the seller's solution. Try to do that by helping the buyer see the difference, not by jamming it down the buyer's throat.

The safety net accomplishes this objective. It comes in several forms:

1. **The qualifying statement.** A qualifying statement is one that is not your personal opinion and is therefore not absolute. In the event that you communicate something inaccurate, qualifying the statement saves you from looking like a liar. The qualifying statement might be something like this:
   - "To the best of my knowledge . . ."
   - "As far as I know . . ."

- ○ "I've been told . . ."
- ○ "Many customers have told us . . ."
- ○ "A recent analyst report stated . . ."

2. **The attributing statement.** Attributing knowledge gives someone else the credit for what you are about to repeat. Not only does this give your buyer a source whereby the buyer can verify whether your statement is correct, but it also implies that you are a knowledgeable seller who keeps up with the latest research. An attributing statement might sound like this:
   - ○ "John Smith with InfoMentis told me that . . ."
   - ○ "Based upon an article in XYZ *Magazine* . . ."
   - ○ "Insight Analyst Group, a lead analyst in our industry, says that . . ."

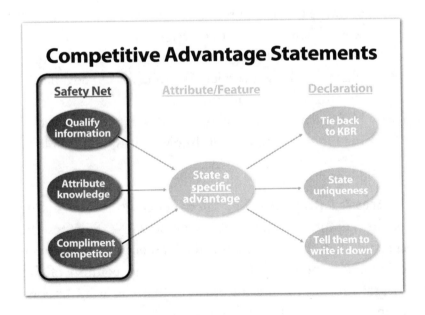

3. **The competitor-compliment statement.** Complimenting the competitor is the most difficult of the three options. It must truly be a compliment without showing evidence of being oblique. When used appropriately, it can be extremely effective. Let's say that you are in competition with a solutions provider that was first-to-market, meaning the other company had the idea first. Though innovative, this idea might have been incomplete in its first generation. Not all buyers are ready to risk using the first-to-market solution because they have low tolerance for risk. In fact many of the most successful companies were not first-to-market; instead, they learned from the first-to-market companies and created an improved solution. Using this example, a competitor compliment might sound like this:

   o "Company A did a great job introducing people to software that didn't require a command line. We were able to leverage that design by . . ."

   o "Company B did an outstanding job by offering free phones with their service. We were able to advance that thinking into offering . . ."

   o "Company C was a pioneer in developing sales training programs; as a result, InfoMentis has been able to advance the thinking by . . ."

The Specific Differentiator The safety net is just the beginning of the competitive advantage statement. Next comes the specific differentiator, which is the element that makes your solution competitively better. The second column of this diagram represents the information that you want to communicate as being the differentiator.

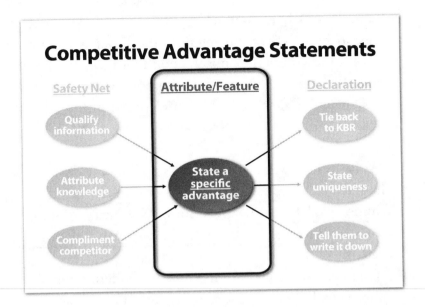

When naming a differentiator, you want to be specific, which allows the buyer to clearly distinguish the difference between you and the other alternatives. Following are examples of nonspecific statements that you want to avoid at all costs:

- "We are the only real provider who has a sound Web strategy."
- "We are number one in the market."
- "We are the only ones who provide true customer service."
- "We have the best sales training in the industry."

These differentiators are far too vague and can appear boastful or arrogant. They fail to offer concrete information to the buyer and, as such, are not helpful. Though a buyer expects a seller to be proud of the solution, the buyer is far more grateful if the seller offers information that helps the buyer make a decision about a solution's superiority. Better examples of specific differentiators are underlined in the following statements:

- "As far as I know, we are the only solution provider that has created voice-activated software that allows you to simply speak to the computer for GPS navigation—just like Captain Picard did. No need for a touch pad to navigate the GPS."
- "Company B did an outstanding job by offering free phones with their service. We were able to advance that thinking into offering conference calling, Webcast scheduling, and collaborative tools with our service."
- "John Neeson has said that InfoMentis has been able to advance the thinking of sales training programs into providing configurable training with change management practices to achieve the desired change in behavior that our clients haven't been able to achieve with stand-alone training."

The Declaration The final part of the competitive statements is the flag, or the definitive action or statement that ties it all together, clearly indicating to the buyer that this is something that should stand out on the list.

Unless the buyer recognizes the clear point, your competitive messaging is useless—just another benefit statement that gets lost in the rhetoric. The declaration makes the solution relevant and "sticky" in three key ways:

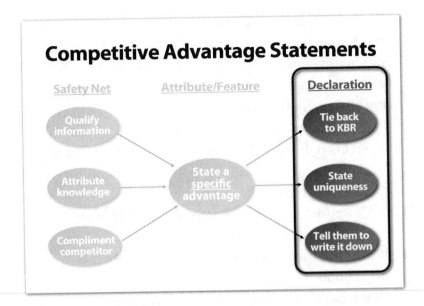

1. **It ties the specific advantage to a key player/key business requirement (KBR), or to key decision criteria.**
   By tying your unique advantage to a key issue or person, you place more weight on the competitive statement than on other statements you may make in the conversation, you appear to have done your homework, and you are helping the buyer choose the best possible solution. You might say:
   - "John, based upon your focus on cost savings, this would be instrumental in cutting your operating costs."
   - "Betty, this would be important based upon your initiatives to improve customer service."
   - "Tom, this piece of our solution ties specifically to your ease-of-use decision criteria."

2. **It demonstrates uniqueness**. It is important to say you are unique if you are unique. Solutions often look and sound the same, so by saying your solution is unique, you will engage people in your conversation. You might introduce uniqueness by saying:

   o "This is unique in the industry because . . ."
   o "This is different from any other alternatives in that it . . ."
   o "We are the only patented solution available today."
   o "The three things that are very different about the design of our solution are . . ."

3. **It asks the buyer to commit this information to memory**. Simply asking a buyer to write information down might sound trite, but it gives the buyer a way to engage in your conversation. This creates stickiness by giving your buyers concrete reminders they can revisit when they reconvene to discuss alternatives. This might sound something like the following:

   o "You might want to make note of this as you compare the alternatives that you are evaluating."
   o "This is a key point in your decision criteria, so you might want to write this down."
   o "John, as this point was specifically on the RFP, you might want to highlight our solution in this area."

Competitive Traps

Creating competitive preference is not something that happens in a single event. It is the process by which the buyer starts to form opinions about the alternatives and with which one the buyer feels most comfortable. Since it is a process, we have to think about ways that we can start to develop preference early and often. Early competitive positioning is largely done through competitive traps.

Establishing Preference by Setting Competitive Traps

As you begin the process of developing preference for your solution and setting traps for the competition, think about the competitive analysis done in Chapter 5. Why would the buyer buy from Competitor 1? Why wouldn't the buyer buy from Competitor 1?

Take that analysis one step further and consider more than just the competitor's product or service. What about the competitor's company as a whole? Its experience within this industry? Its community awards and recognition? Its location? Its corporate culture? Its approach to services? A buyer might consider dozens of factors beyond the product or service.

Consider as well the behavior of the people on the competitor's selling team. How do they approach a sale? Do they discount early? How does their competitive positioning come across to a buyer? Are they as experienced as you and your team?

The only way to gain this insight is to ask your customers (buyers who choose your solution) about their buying experience. What did they like about the competition? What could the competition have done better? And ask the same questions again and again of each customer; eventually you can develop an integrated image of the buyers' perception of your competitors.

Armed with this information, consider how you can set competitive traps through your competitive advantages.

Larry set the following competitive trap when meeting with Hargrove:

Jenny Fine from Greencoat would tell you that what was still missing in their system was the ability to inspect deals. They didn't connect the dots between sales training and validation of data entry. They had assumed that because they trained the sales teams, their data would be accurate. The trouble was: the data wasn't. What our solution provided was the methodology questions for validation at the source of data entry. Instead of the reps entering when the deal would close, for example, the close date is calculated based on the answers to the methodology questions and sales cycle historical statistics. This insight into deals allowed the sales reps to execute in the sales cycle consistently; it also allowed proactive adjustments based on the methodology. Managers then had time to coach and strategize on how to win instead of inspecting deals for accuracy. I don't know how important that is to your vice president of sales, but it certainly affected Greencoat's ability to impact deals and win.

Preempting Competitive Traps

Of course, the flip side of setting competitive traps is that you will also have to respond to competitive traps. The best way to handle a competitor's trap is to simply avoid having it occur in the first place. The more you think through competitive strategies and evaluate the pros and cons of your solution versus other alternatives, the more you will develop an ability to avoid traps altogether.

If you are thorough and objective during your competitive assessment, you will identify some key opportunities for the competition to set you up, especially in the category of why a buyer would not buy from you. The longer and more thorough you can make this list, the more traps you can avoid.

Let's say your organization is new to the manufacturing industry. You do not have many manufacturing customers or manufacturing references. Your Competitive Map would certainly reference this as a reason that a buyer might not buy from you.

You can preempt any competitive trap your competition might set in a variety of ways:

1. Bring it up early to your potential Coach. And do it before your competition mentions it. Ask your Coach if this will be a deal killer. If your lack of industry experience will kill the deal, you will know not to invest too much time or resources. On the other hand, this could be an opportunity qualifier. If your Coach lets you know that your limited penetration into the market is irrelevant, the competitor's trap might even seem petty when the competitor uses it to try to gain momentum.

2. If you want to wait to address the issue and test your competition, inform your Coach that your competitors have been known to bring up references as an issue. Ask your Coach to let you know if this happens so that you can address any concerns directly.

3. Focus on how your organization prepared to enter the manufacturing market, and be direct in relaying these experiences.
   - Tell success stories regarding best practices from other industries that can be shared with manufacturing.
   - Share the expertise of the team members your company hired when they decided to enter the manufacturing market.

- ○ Highlight the manufacturing customer advisory board that has directed your company in this new venture.
- ○ Tell the buyer about any certifications your company has earned through manufacturing governing bodies.

Responding to Competitive Traps and Handling Objections

Responding to traps refers to a process for answering questions or objections that clarifies the difference between what the buyer thinks is true and what is actually true. In some cases, the trap that was set might actually reflect the truth, but preparing for tough questions, objections, and traps will help you gain more control over the impression that you want to leave.

For instance, let's say that you missed your targeted revenue last quarter. Your competitor may want to use that information to create an impression in the buyer's mind that your business is in trouble, that fewer people are buying your solution, and that your financial future is unsound. You can respond to this trap by using the truth to clarify the gray area created by the competition.

In this case, if you missed your numbers, you missed your numbers. But were the numbers too high? Did the company still grow over all? Was your performance better than the competition's? Was there a merger? Was there a divestiture? Did you sunset a solution?

A number of valid business reasons might cause a company to miss its numbers. However, it does not indicate that the company is in trouble. If you want to answer these fair questions with business maturity and not competitive panic, preparing for these types of setups will help your responses sound confident and convincing.

Thinking through ways that the competition might try to trap you will achieve the following:

○ **Help keep the topic focused on how your solution addresses the pains and key business requirements.** The competition might throw random points into the mix, but if they are not relevant for the buyer, those points are easy to diffuse. This won't stop competitors from using traps, but it will make it easier for you to discount their importance and make the competition appear unfocused on the issues at hand.

○ **Provide a way to avoid or defer deal-breaking issues.** If a buyer has stated that certain criteria are require-ments for an evaluation, then you can think through all the competitive traps that might suggest you do not meet those requirements. For instance, if the company requires that you have at least three customers in its industry and you have only three, should you reveal this up front? While you meet the criteria, you certainly are not thriving in the market. Identifying deal breakers up front can allow you to gracefully exit the competition before you spend time and resources on a deal that is bound to die. And if you decide to proceed nonetheless, you can do so with increased knowledge and a plan for addressing those points of weakness.

○ **Provide an opportunity to set the record straight and build competitive advantage.** Preparation and thorough handling of traps and objections can be instrumental in building the buyer's confidence in you. When you are prepared, you show that you can stay on top of what is going on and what is being said in your industry. Your buyer will appreciate your professional "calm and cool."

At the same time, you can deflate the buyer's confidence in your competitor.

When presented with a competitive trap, always get clarification before you respond. Most sellers have a tendency to start talking right away, which generally turns into a ramble that unravels your credibility quite quickly. A good rule of thumb for responding to any tough question/objection/trap is as follows:

1. **Pause.** Make sure that you have heard and understand the question.
2. **Probe and/or paraphrase.** If the question is unclear or vague, ask questions to gain clarity into what the buyer is really asking. If the question is asked in a somewhat disjointed fashion, paraphrase it back to the buyer to make sure you understood exactly what the buyer is really asking. This also gives you more time to think about how you want to answer this objection—especially if it is one you hadn't anticipated.
3. **Provide a response (and confirm).** Answer the buyer's question and ask for confirmation that you have addressed all concerns.

Let's take a look at how this exchange might actually occur:

Anna asks Larry, "Why is your solution so expensive to implement?"

Larry pauses and then asks for clarification, "Help me understand what you mean by expensive. Are you talking about price, implementation costs, or total cost of ownership?"

Anna says, "I have just heard that your implementation is the most expensive on the market, and I wanted to understand why that is."

Larry then responds, "I have not heard that feedback from customers. In fact, the cost of implementation has never been a concern, especially when our customers see the integration of our solution. We use a highly defined implementation methodology, which gives us visibility into project progress and costs at all times. Our implementation time frames and costs are in line with what is expected for this type of project. As you know, we do offer quite a few other solutions, so buyers will often request additional solutions from our team because they are so happy with our products. But when compared head-to-head with other solutions, our customers tell us that our integrated software package actually is less expensive than the combined cost of the compartmentalized pieces on the market."

Let's look at what happened during this exchange. Anna asked a question that was likely provided to her by one of Larry's competitors. Larry knew this because when he asked Anna to clarify, she was unable to provide any real personal frame of reference. Larry took the opportunity to neutralize the trap and turn it to his company's advantage by saying that buyers actually continue to request services because the solution and organization are strong.

Let's consider how this might have unfolded had the answer to the probing question been different:

Anna asks Larry, "Why is your solution so expensive to implement?"

Larry pauses and then asks for clarification: "Help me understand what you mean by expensive. Are you talking about price, implementation costs, or total cost of ownership?"

Anna answers, "A colleague of mine shared his implementation costs with me. When compared to the quotes I am getting and the cost of our current solution, this cost seems excessive."

Larry then replies: "Without knowing your colleague, I can only speculate. There are many reasons why implementation costs exceed estimates. It could be that your colleague had a change in scope. The company could have had executive turnover. They could have had a staffing issue that required more resources from us than originally planned. Perhaps they requested additional solutions. The estimate we have given you is based on what you have provided us to date as it relates to staffing and talent. In fact, 90 percent of our implementations are on time and under budget. This is because we use a highly defined implementation methodology, which gives us visibility into project progress and costs at all times."

[pause]

"I just want to confirm: did my answer address your question?"

Responding to objections can be scary. The seller has to determine quickly whether the buyer is asking a question out of curiosity, because the issue could be a barrier to winning the sale, or whether the question is a competitive trap set by another seller. If the former, the seller does not have to provide as thorough a response than if the latter is the reason.

The following are key things to remember about objections and tough questions:

○ **Don't rush to respond.** If you answer before the question has been asked completely, you risk sounding rude and desperate. As well, you might not be answering the right question.

○ **Make sure you understand.** As an objection or a tough question arises, take time to make sure you really understand the buyer's concern. Ask for clarification to your satisfaction before providing an answer. Try to determine whether the buyer is asking out of curiosity, because the issue is a barrier to entry, or because of a trap set by one of your competitors.

○ **Be concise and clear.** Once you understand what is being asked, answer with clarity and succinctness. If your answer rambles on, it quickly loses its credibility.

DO . . .	DO NOT . . .
Acknowledge similarities and place little focus on them.	Use absolute language without a safety net.
Talk about your advantages, not the competitor's weaknesses.	Refer to the competitor by name unless you are complimenting the competitor.
Respond calmly to competitive traps with patience.	Get defensive when presented with a competitive trap.
Be specific and use simple language and easy-to-understand examples. Don't leave it up to the buyer to have to interpret what you're saying.	Overcomplicate your message by using complex terms and acronyms that will not resonate with the buyer.
Make your competitive statements relative to things that are important to the buyer.	Underestimate the competition. You should always assume that the competitors have a strong competitive game plan.
Plan for competitive advantages that you want to convey and practice delivering your competitive advantage statements ahead of time.	Wing it.

Finally, do your homework. Competitive information changes all the time. Solution providers frequently come out with new products, new solutions, and new references that are unknown or unfamiliar to you. They fix problems in existing solutions. They come up with new rebuttals that put your strategy on the defensive, or they uncover new information about you so that they can outmaneuver you.

Remember that competitive information changes all of the time, so you have to constantly do your homework to know who and what you are up against. Check the websites of your competition. When you win a deal, ask your new customers what they liked and disliked about the competition.

CHAPTER 9

High-Yield Questions to Support Your Strategy

> "Success hinges on collecting, evaluating, and executing to bring the best new concepts to fruition."
>
> —Pat Byrne, Managing Director, Accenture

My husband and I recently experienced the painstaking process of trying to buy a car from someone who asked the wrong questions and misinterpreted my answers. Prior to visiting dealerships, I had investigated my options and knew what kind of cars I would consider buying. I knew from previous experience that car shopping is rough on a good day. Every salesperson knows what is right for the car buyer, telling the buyer about features and benefits that are irrelevant to the buyer. Salespeople want to keep the buyers in the lot as long as possible to prevent them from going to another dealership.

I came across one salesman who asked several questions about our situation: why we were looking at a new car, what car I was currently driving, what we do for a living, the number of children we have, and how old our children are. I was pleasantly surprised. He was taking an interest and considering what we may like or dislike in a car.

And then he spun into a sales pitch about how much time we spend in the car and how many meals my children eat on the run and why the cup holders and tray tables and attached trash can would be invaluable to me as a mom with three kids in sports. His pitch was at least twenty-five minutes long and totally irrelevant: I have never allowed my children to eat in the car because the car becomes a traveling trash can and because it prevents face-to-face communication over meals, which I consider to be invaluable family time.

Not wanting to be rude, I eventually tuned out completely and tried to figure out some way to get out of the dealership. Although he asked several questions and listened to my answers, he heard what was familiar to him and *assumed he had the answers*.

In fact, he asked the wrong questions. Had he asked a High-Yield Question, he could have saved time and turned our interaction into a sale. But more often than not, salespeople simply ask a long list of questions hoping to uncover critical information (this is their silver bullet). When a seller tries to ask all the questions on the list, the meeting begins to feel like an interview, or even worse, an interrogation. The buyer begins to feel drained and empty during the meeting because it's a one-way conversation. And the seller is busy interpreting the answers before moving on to the next question. When the buyer does all the giving of information but gets nothing back in return, it may feel unfair to the buyer, who leaves the meeting feeling empty.

This is not the dynamic that the seller wants to establish early in a relationship. Instead, sellers want the meeting to be upbeat, jointly valuable, and collaborative in nature. Developing and using High-Yield Questions help the seller establish strong rapport with the buyers and build credibility while gaining insight into them, all of which can create a competitive advantage all by itself.

By now, you are probably wondering what High-Yield Questions are. High-Yield Questions are those that uncover the most amount of information using the fewest number of questions. Let's look at an example.

Imagine that you are a police sketch artist listening as a victim describes a suspect. You have created a sketch based on the description the victim has provided. As you complete the first sketch, you want to know how close the sketch is to the victim's memory of the suspect. Knowing that early sketches are never 100 percent accurate, which of the following questions would uncover the most information using the fewest number of questions?

"Is this right?"

or

"What about this picture would you change?"

"Is this right?" can uncover only two pieces of information: either the sketch is correct (highly unlikely), or it needs

work, meaning you will have to continue asking questions to uncover what is incorrect about the sketch.

Asking the second question—"What about this picture would you change?"—immediately offers the victim the opportunity to begin discussing specifics of what needs to be changed. In other words, it provides the greatest amount of information in the shortest amount of time.

In any meeting with a buyer, your goal is to advance to the next stage. High-Yield Questions are designed to allow you to uncover the information you need to advance, which will generally fall into five categories:

1. **Confirmation.** Confirmation means that you have confirmed what you believe to be true.
2. **Perception.** Perception is reality. Everyone has opinions as to situations and how they should be addressed. Understanding preconceived ideas, especially of key individuals, is important. Knowing how they view a situation and how they would fix it lets you see where you have opportunities for alignment or where you might need to change someone's mind-set.
3. **Factual.** Using information that has quantitative measurement is more powerful than using vague references. For instance, knowing that the buyer needs to decrease expenses by 8 percent is better than just knowing that the buyer needs to significantly reduce expenses. By uncovering factual information, you might have an opportunity to advance to the next stage by showing how your solution addresses the buyer's needs.
4. **Impact.** To understand the cause and effect of current situations, you need to know the business impact and who is affected. When someone describes a situation, you should also be thinking about how this situation affects other parts of the organization. Or, said differently, what bad thing will happen if this is never fixed? If the answer is not significant, you may not have a good buying situation. If the buyers don't know the answer, you may need to speak to someone else in the organization who does know so that you can determine whether your solution is a good fit, and whether you should advance.
5. **Commitment.** As you gain insight and the buyer starts to ask things of you, you want to start to ask for some commitment in return for your efforts, or as I would say,

you should request a trade exchange. This begins to set expectations with the buyer that this is a fair relationship that is moving forward.

After you have considered what types of information you need before you can advance, you can develop High-Yield Questions that will provide you with this information.

Imagine that you are an advertising/public-relations firm making a sales call to a large multinational training and consulting firm. You want to learn more about the buyer's perspective on competitiveness. You might want to know the answers to the following questions:

1. Who are your largest competitors?
2. How do their solutions stack up to yours?
3. How does their market share compare to yours?
4. Do they have a strong sales organization?
5. What are they doing that is effective?
6. How are you beating them?

These are just six of a long list of questions meant to uncover pertinent information about the buyer's competitors. In fact, buyers might be concerned with any number of an endless list of issues surrounding their competitors. But instead of asking a stream of questions, let the buyer lead you by asking a High-Yield Question, such as, "What are the things that are prevalent on your mind relative to your competitive environment?"

Notice that this question gives the seller the opportunity to gain insight into the buyer's perception, and it also provides the buyer with an opportunity to answer the six questions just presented.

The answers to a High-Yield Question will give you insight into the buyer's *perceptions,* as well as *factual* data, the people *impacted,* and the buyer's *commitment* to this area of business growth or concern. You will likely have to ask some additional questions (I call them "Layering Questions") based on the buyer's answers to your High-Yield Question—such as how many, how long, what happens if this is never fixed—but already you have narrowed the list of questions drastically.

The information you uncover when asking High-Yield and Layering Questions can be used to continue your Collaboration Map, which serves as a reflection of all the conversations you have had with the buyer and a picture by which you can *confirm* your understanding of the business challenge the buyer is facing.

In addition, by letting the buyer lead the conversation, you are maximizing your time together instead of asking twenty questions, which may or may not be about variables that are important to the buyer. You have a very short window of time to establish credibility, especially when you are meeting with more senior managers or executives. In fact, executives tell us that you have less than two minutes to establish your credibility in the mind of an executive. If you start rattling off generic questions, the executives know that you put little thought into preparing for the meeting. Remember that the executive has no interest in educating you; rather, the executive is curious to learn something from you.

But if you open with a High-Yield Question, you create an immediate opportunity to establish credibility and pull critical information from the buyer. Consider, for instance, the different impression you would create if you asked a

High-Yield Question that pulls from your experience instead of rattling off a long list of questions. Imagine that you are calling on a shipping company. You have experience in this industry, so in advance of the meeting, you brainstorm for High-Yield Questions that are a basis for exchange, that serve as an introduction to your experience and credibility, and that generate a ton of information in the shortest amount of time. You might ask something like this:

> *In working with others in the shipping business, we have helped folks like Shipping International and Cosco look at ways to provide faster, high-quality, competitive shipping services. What types of initiatives do you have in place for continued service improvement?*

In this example of a High-Yield "opener" (a High-Yield Question used to open the meeting), you accomplished three things:

1. You stated an indisputable fact ("In working with others in the shipping business") that established your experience and immediately built rapport between you and the buyer.
2. You referenced a client success story ("we have helped folks like Shipping International and Cosco look at ways to provide faster, high quality, competitive shipping services"). In doing so, you might have piqued the buyer's interest with two client names that reference success in competitive shipping services, which quickly builds a second layer of credibility.
3. You asked a High-Yield Question ("What types of initiatives do you have in place for continued service improvement?"). You have set the groundwork and let the

buyers know that you likely understand their business. Now they have an opportunity to share their initiatives. Because you have disclosed information about yourself, you have opened the door for the buyers to put on a thinking cap and start providing you with information that might help you advance.

If you fail to prepare High-Yield Questions, you would be left asking questions such as, "How is business going for you?" This reflects little thought, fails to establish you as an expert, and hardly shows the buyer that you have any knowledge of the industry at all. Instead, the buyer will think you are trying to wing it, which is not at all impressive.

As you plan your interactions with the buyer, constantly think about what you need to support your strategy, or at least advance your position to the next stage in the buying process or to advance your relationship with the buyers. Information needed to advance might include:

o A better understanding of how the buyers are currently operating or the challenges that have led them to look for a different solution,

o A better understanding of what they consider viable alternatives to addressing their business needs, and/or

o A better understanding of the key people involved and any preconceived notions they may have about solutions.

When you think of the questions that need to be answered before you can advance, the list might be long. With High-Yield Questions, though, you can create questions that provide the dual purpose of supporting your strategy and setting the stage for buyers to come to their own conclusions about your solution's superiority, which is much more powerful than jamming messages down their throats.

Developing the Right Questions

Our clients often ask us to provide a magical list of questions they should ask buyers. In short, they are looking for a silver bullet. This silver bullet is just that—a myth in the world of selling. Because each buyer is different, I cannot provide such a list; I can, however, provide a formula to help you determine what the questions should be. This formula has several stages:

Early in the buying process, you reflect on your strategy—Frontal, Flanking, Fragment, or Defend—and what information you need to advance. Remember that if you have chosen a Flanking Strategy, you should not ask questions that illuminate the possibility that your solution might not win in a head-to-head competition.

Considering the information you need to uncover before you can advance, ask yourself this question: *What is the best possible information I could receive from the buyer?* In other words, if you could determine exactly how the buyer would answer your questions, what would that answer sound like?

Finally, take a shot at creating a question that would lead to that answer.

Before asking the buyer this question, first test it on someone who knows the buyer, such as a fellow sales team member. Adjust the question accordingly depending on the answer you get.

When preparing to meet with Anna to discuss her sales effectiveness software needs, Larry first reflects on his strategy. One of the differentiators that makes Outstanding

Options such a strong contender in this market is that it provides its users with sales methodology intelligence to determine the health of a deal or account, not just the ability to enter data about it. As such, Larry has chosen a Flanking Strategy: he wants to change the rules of this evaluation by understanding the business impact of Hargrove's sales effectiveness challenges so that he can create a link between his solution and Hargrove's business impact.

Before he can advance, Larry needs to know how Hargrove is impacted when sales representatives don't enter their sales data according to their methodology. In other words, he wants to know the impact of not following their sales methodology.

In a perfect world, Anna would tell Larry that because sales teams and managers are very inconsistent on sales execution, the forecast data are not reliable, causing a significant amount of reworking to massage the numbers for Wall Street. Executives just don't have the confidence in the teams to believe the numbers in the system.

Initially, Larry came up with a question—"What is the impact of not having an accurate forecast?" But this question seemed a little obvious and self-serving, as if he were being condescending. The impact was, of course, negative, which Anna had clearly already considered. As well, it wouldn't necessarily lead to his desired response.

Larry adjusted his question—"What have you found to be the reasons that sales managers do forecast calls and rework the numbers every month instead of just using the numbers in your current sales software solution?"

In asking this question, Larry sets the stage for Anna to give him the desired response, which in turn allows Larry an opportunity to solidify his strategy and advance to the next

	Content
Information needed to advance	
Who would know	
Desired response	
Formulate question	
Test and adjust *If the original question can be answered without giving the information needed, it should be adjusted to achieve your goals.*	

stage by showing Anna how his solution would merge all the systems into one integrated solution.

Let's look at another example.

Larry is finally meeting with Terry, a financial analyst at Hargrove who might have excellent insight into the financial outcomes of Hargrove's current solution. Larry knows that analysts are also a good source of information for identifying the executives and decision makers within an organization. But before he can advance, he decides to give himself the following objectives:

1. Assess Terry's influence
2. Gain insight into others who would influence this evaluation
3. Learn about Hargrove's current environment and its challenges from Terry's perspective
4. Set up a follow-up meeting with influencers

As you can see, Larry is working on rounding out his Influence Map. To advance, he needs better information about the people who vote.

The first objective may be the trickiest when it comes to questions. Larry cannot simply ask the financial analyst if he is influential. Instead, he might ask:

- "What evaluations have you been involved with before?"
- "What went well, and what would you change in future evaluations?"
- "What characteristics do you look for in a strategic partner?"
- "Who are your favorite vendors to work with and why?"

To gain insight (Objective #2), he might ask:

- "Who initiated or sponsored this evaluation and why?" Or, "What caused you to look for a new solution?"
- "Who is most impacted by the current challenges?"
- "How will you make a decision, or what criteria will tell you a good solution from a marginal solution?"

To learn about the current environment (Objective #3), he might ask:

- "What are the key challenges of the current environment?"
- "What works well?"
- "What happens if you leave it as it is?"
- "Who is involved in maintaining and using the current environment?"

And for follow-up (Objective #4), he might ask:

○ "Will you set up a follow-up meeting with others who would be involved so that I can better understand their issues and introduce them to our solution?" (This is also a good question to use when you are testing for a Coach on the buying team. A Coach is someone who wants you to win, so if Terry is willing to set up this meeting, Larry might be on his way to discovering a Coach.)

○ "What type of process do you typically use to evaluate?" (This is a good question to set up a potential Joint Evaluation Plan or to collaborate on a Joint Evaluation Plan.)

○ "What do you see as next steps?" (Larry is not pushing the next steps on the buyer here because he wants to see if Terry has thought about what would be best to advance; again here is another test of the person with whom he is speaking.)

All of these, and more, are valid High-Yield Questions. In the course of normal conversations, Larry would have the opportunity to ask these questions if he planned in advance.

Testing and Improving Questions

In the previous section, we brainstormed about the questions we would like to have answered. Now that we know what kind of insight that we are looking for, how do we take those questions and improve them?

Let's go back to Larry's objectives when meeting with Terry:

1. Assess Terry's influence
2. Gain insight into others who would influence this evaluation
3. Learn about Hargrove's current environment and its challenges from Terry's perspective
4. Set up a follow-up meeting with influencers

Let's first consider the order of the objectives. Remember that buyers are wary of sales representatives who come across as arrogant or care more about their own product or service than the buyer's business. With that in mind, Larry does not want to lead with questions about influence; instead, he can begin by understanding the environment and needs.

Here are the raw questions we came up with earlier. How might we test and improve those?

- "What are the key challenges of the current environment?"
- "What works well?"
- "What happens if you leave it as it is?"
- "Who is involved in maintaining and using the current environment?"

Let's look at the first one: "What are the key challenges of the current environment?"

This seems like a good conversation starter. It is also an open-ended question. How could it be improved?

1. Larry runs the risk of asking a question that is too open-ended. If asked this question, the buyer might begin to talk about staffing issues, employee morale, old equipment, or outdated technology. The list of possible answers is endless, and while Larry wants to understand as many dynamics as possible, he really wants to focus on the issues that his software solution can address.

2. This question does not establish Larry's credibility, and an opener is the first chance that Larry has to establish credibility.

Incorporating these two critiques, the question might evolve into something like this:

> *In working with other finance teams, I have found that most, just like you, spend an extraordinary amount of time questioning the validity of the sales forecast from their systems. In fact, the amount of work that is done every month to rework the numbers is very frustrating. What do you believe are the key challenges for you in this area?*

Notice that Larry's question not only requests insight into a specific arena, but it is also posed in such a way that it introduces Larry's experience with other finance departments and conversations with others inside Terry's organization.

Let's look at one more: "Who is involved in this effort to make it work every month?"

Because this is a "who" question, Larry should automatically think about this as an opportunity to gain factual and impact insight. This is an opportunity to help Larry start to piece together levels of influence. Consider how he might follow up on this question:

o "Who is impacted the most every month when the fore-cast is wrong?"
o "What happens if this is never fixed?"
o "How much time do those who make it happen and those who are impacted spend validating the data?"
o "How hard is it to really gain the right insight into the status of a deal?"
o "How much time do they spend reworking the data after they inspect or validate it with the reps?"
o "If they had accurate data in the system to begin with, what could they be doing that they are not doing today?"
o "What do you believe are the key challenges for you in this area?"
o "As you look at those in the business areas and those responsible for maintaining systems, help me to under-stand how the current environment impacts them."

The ability to formulate High-Yield Questions through-out the process is key in tying all the pieces together. You need the right questions to reveal business issues and impact to create your Collaboration Map. You need the right ques-tions to determine your Influence Map. You need the right questions to create the Competitive Map that enables you to select your strategy to win. Once you have your strategy to win, you need the right questions to continue to advance your strategy by uncovering information about perception, impact, facts, commitment, and confirmation.

Patience is mandatory in order to employ High-Yield Questions. The process of uncovering the information you need by asking just the right questions might feel very slow, as though the competition might creep in, speed things up, and gain a competitive advantage. Remember that you must go slowly to go fast. By taking the time to develop High-Yield Questions, you show your buyers that you are

1. Listening closely as opposed to just waiting for your turn to talk again
2. Helping them by finding the parts of your solution that are applicable to their business need
3. Curious about their specific challenges

CHAPTER 10

Your Call Plan

> "Poor execution ruins superior plans. Superior execution saves mediocre plans."
>
> —Donald G. Krause, author of *The Art of War for Executives: Ancient Knowledge for Today's Business Professional* and *The Way of the Leader: Leadership Principles of Sun Tzu and Confucius*

The last few chapters have dealt with some essential but admittedly isolated topics related to sales execution. We now move toward putting this together so that you can execute consistently on every call with the buyer and advance in the process while generating preference for your solution. We do this by using a Call Plan, the string that ties it all together. In using a Call Plan—whether it be during a face-to-face meeting with the buyer or over the phone— you have an opportunity to make sure that the words that you use will create a good impression about you, your team, and your company. In other words, this is where the rubber meets the road. Without a Call Plan, you run the risk of poor execution. With a Call Plan, you have an integrated, intentional meeting that uses High-Yield Questions, competitive traps, and competitive positioning that allows the seller to advance by measuring when and whether the buyer and seller are on the same page.

A Call Plan is, in essence, an outline for a meeting with a buyer and is used solely by the sales team so that thoughts are organized, expectations are identified, and outcomes are defined before engaging with the buyer. Though the Call Plan is an internal document, it has the benefit of strengthening the buyer's perception of the seller. A Call Plan lets the buyer know that you are organized and prepared and not simply shooting from the hip. In the buyer's mind, a crisp, concise, and clear meeting indicates an organized implementation, which creates feelings of security in the buyer.

Likewise, having a well-thought-out plan will help you and your team focus on making each event count, moving the decision in your favor. All too often, teams show up at meetings with little preparation as to what the outcomes and expectations are and what it is they are specifically being asked to do. In those cases, people inadvertently say and do things that create awkward situations, which creates a sense of trepidation with the buyer.

Proper preparation will create synergy and allow the team to do the best job possible. Having a game plan that outlines the outcomes and everyone's role in a sales call yields stronger results. Leveraging each team member is critical, as is determining who will be responsible for communicating specific messages and asking questions. This can serve you well as you try to gather and validate information throughout the process.

The Call Plan:

1. Defines the agenda
2. Pinpoints where you are in the buying process
3. Specifies meeting logistics
4. Reminds the seller of the strategy and why it was chosen
5. Defines the buyer's business issues
6. Establishes the buyer's expectations
7. Clarifies your outcomes
8. Identifies the attendees and their roles from both the buyer's team and the seller's team
9. Clarifies the information the seller will convey
10. Includes the High-Yield Questions the seller will ask in order to collect information needed to advance
11. Specifies which team members will set competitive traps
12. Predicts what objections the buyer might have, as well as what the seller's response should be
13. Outlines what will be done prior to the meeting

The Agenda

To a large extent, the Call Plan is the agenda. We suggest also creating an agenda that is distributed to the buyer that simply addresses the outcomes for the meeting from the buyer's perspective. This is a courteous gesture, but moreover, by distributing this portion of the Call Plan, the seller gives the buyer the opportunity to do the following:

1. Alert the seller if the agenda does not meet the buyer's objectives
2. Provide input into the agenda if they want to discuss something different from or in addition to the current plan
3. Confirm the meeting is still taking place
4. Discuss other attendees who would make the meeting more productive

When you are preparing the agenda, anticipate the buyer's frame of mind for the call by asking yourself and your team the following questions:

- "What relationship do I have with each person who will be attending?"
- "Have the buyers met with the competition prior to meeting with us?"
- "What might they have seen or heard already?"
- "Over what time frame have they had meetings with the competition?"
- "Where are we in the overall evaluation process?"

Depending on the answers to these questions, you can then "guesstimate" the buyer's potential frame of mind and develop an agenda to optimize your time. Setting the agenda also helps you define the rest of the Call Plan, which you will *not* share with the buyer.

Pinpointing Where You Are in the Buying Process

When we discussed the buying process in Chapter 2, "The Gap Between Buyers and Sellers," you learned that the sales team earns the respect of the buyer by addressing what the buyer needs in order to make a decision. You, the sales professional, must align with the buyer. Every Call Plan pinpoints the buyer's position in the buying process, which lets the team know how to behave and what level of respect the sales team might have earned. The sales team is therefore able to set expectations and outcomes that are realistic and aligned with the buying process.

The Meeting Logistics

Have you ever been preparing for a meeting and discovered that you don't have the address for the meeting, don't have the conference room name, don't know the number for the conference call that is about to take place, have not been told the dress code, or have no idea who is supposed to bring the projector?

It sounds so basic, but the meeting logistics are often overlooked, which inserts a great deal of risk into the process. Just imagine how the buyer will perceive you if you

- Are late
- Call to confess that you do not have the address
- Dress inappropriately
- Arrive unprepared, without markers, the projector, handouts, or business cards

191

You get the picture, and you are probably cringing, thinking of the times you have arrived at meetings without your business cards or dressed in the wrong attire. Dropping the ball on meeting logistics happens all the time. In fact, I once heard of a sales representative who flew to Nashville to meet a buyer. Trouble was, the meeting was supposed to be in the buyer's Memphis office!

Your Strategy

Consistent execution means that you constantly remind yourself and your fellow sales team members of your strategy to win. By consistently linking the strategy to the actions, all sellers in the meeting will know which activities will support the strategy. If your strategy is to flank your competition, you know you need to change the rules. Early in the buying process, your Call Plan might focus on identifying the current rules, as well as what message you can send to change the rules. For example, Larry chose a Flanking Strategy that would focus on sales effectiveness rather than on time to integrate the solution.

The Buyer's Business Issues

By attaching your Collaboration Map to the Call Plan, you compress the amount of time your sales team needs to get up to speed on the buyer. (In fact, you might want to share the Collaboration Map with the buyer during every interaction.) As you remember from previous chapters, the Collaboration

Map shows the buyer that you have done your homework and are interested in the buyer's business. As well, you communicate the buyer's challenges to the sales team so the sales team can focus the meeting on business issues that are relevant to the buyer.

The Buyer's Expectations

Your team's best interest is to know the expectations of all players at the meeting, especially the key players; influencers; decision makers; executive sponsors; people with preference for you, such as your Coach; and people with preference for others. Knowing their expectations allows your team to meet and exceed those expectations, to appear focused on the buyer instead of the seller, and to earn the right to advance.

Remember John of Solution Brokers from Part 1? John is the poor fellow who walked into a meeting with Hargrove, only to see seven new faces on the buyer's team. Had John considered the buyer's expectations for the meeting, he would have known that the buying team would include new members who would need a recap of the solution. John might have salvaged the deal had he considered the buyer's expectations for the meeting (fortunately for Larry, he didn't!).

Your Outcomes

Having defined measurable outcomes causes a team to behave in such a way as to achieve the optimal results in the qualification process. If you don't have well-defined outcomes, measuring the success of the call is impossible, inconsistent, and risky.

Defining the minimal and optimal outcomes for each meeting creates a benchmark for you to answer this question: what is the very minimum that needs to happen to justify the time and resources that you spend on the meeting? Being in the same place as when you started means that you have not advanced in any significant way. In other words, you have wasted your time by failing to make sure that you advance your objectives.

Your outcomes should follow the S.M.A.R.T. formula:

○ **Specific.** The objective must be concrete.
○ **Measurable.** Was the objective met? If you cannot answer this question with yes or no, it is not measurable.
○ **Aggressive.** Can this objective be met?
○ **Realistic.** Is it realistic that this objective be met at this stage in the game?
○ **Time-bound.** When must this objective be met in order to consider the meeting successful?

Often the hardest part of this formula is setting outcomes that are measurable. Regularly, we hear sales teams say that the objective of a call is to improve the seller's relationship with the buyer. But how will the seller know if this has happened? Improving a relationship cannot be quantified or answered with an absolute yes or no. A sales rep might say the relationship was improved, but how does he know? Here are some examples of measurable objectives:

○ The buyer introduces the seller to the executive sponsor prior to the end of the meeting.
○ The buyer coordinates the next meeting with the decision maker.
○ The buyer gives the seller confidential information it has not yet disclosed.

In setting outcomes, sales teams often fail to set aggressive goals. Instead, they identify information that they can collect by asking just one question—information that the buyer would provide to any seller. The seller might want to

○ Gather information about the buyer's business,
○ Confirm the buyer's goals, and
○ Confirm the buyer's time frame.

These are weak, minimal outcomes. Goals can help the seller advance if they are a bit more aggressive, such as these:

○ The potential Coach collaborates on the Collaboration Map and suggests other key players who should be included in the validation. This helps confirm that the potential Coach is indeed a Coach.
○ The buyer agrees to help create the Joint Evaluation Plan so that the buying and selling teams can manage the plan dates and move toward the deadline.

Once a seller has established aggressive minimal outcomes, then the seller can define the optimal outcomes. Though a seller might not reach its optimal outcomes, the seller should know what the best possible outcomes are so that the sales team knows when the entire buying team seems to have preference. Optimal outcomes might include these:

○ The Coach tells the seller how to win.
○ The buyer proactively suggests a meeting with the decision maker and executive sponsor to validate the resources and time frames identified in the Joint Evaluation Plan.

When determining your outcomes, you also want to consider a buyer's expectations, how much time the buyer has, and how much time you have. This allows you to maximize the time you spend.

Identifying Attendees

Looking at the Influence Map, you might ask these questions of yourself and others on your sales team:

○ *Do we need anyone else at the meeting in addition to who is currently invited?* Perhaps someone on your sales team has a strong relationship with one of the attendees from the buying team. Adding attendees from your sales team might help you advance.
○ *What role will the attendees play in the meeting?*
○ *How should the seller resources align with the buyers attending?*

These are the questions you need answered when you are discussing the attendees and their roles to ensure you have all the right resources available to allow you to achieve your outcomes and advance your position.

Have you ever been in a meeting when your team accidentally ignored someone in the meeting who was important? Or had an important person walk into a meeting and go unacknowledged? Or have you had several team members pay too much attention to one attendee while ignoring the others?

Worse yet, have you had team members answer questions about price that conflict with information someone else has already given them? Or had a sales rep commit to something that is not possible?

If you discuss your Call Plan, the attendees, and their responsibilities in advance, these accidents will be avoided. Looking at the following chart, you can see that the context of the call might change depending on the people attending the meeting. Are they executives, middle management, or project professionals?

By knowing all this information, as well as the hot buttons for each of these people, you can better assess their time frame and personal agenda and determine the "conversational context." That is, you can determine what conversations you should have during the meeting.

Because words matter, this chart becomes handy in helping sellers select the right words in their messages. If you are speaking with an operational professional, for instance, then you know that you are talking to a person who has been assigned to a project or initiative and is responsible for executing on the initiative. This person is spending already-approved funds and is measuring the results of initiatives. Organizational professionals usually like to discuss price,

Responsibilities	Conversational Context		
	What They Like to Discuss	**Their Time Frame**	**Their Proposal & Professional Agenda**
Executives			
1. Establish corporate vision			
2. Establish strategic initiatives	Results	Future	Legacy
3. Establish corporate policies to manage and mitigate risk			
Middle Management			
1. Implement initiatives for strategies	Cost	Present	Success
2. Develop budgets			
3. Assign resources to projects			
Operations/Professionals			
1. Executive initiatives			
2. Spend funds	Price	Past	Survival
3. Measure results			

and their concerns or interests are usually based on what has happened to them in the past. Their personal agenda is usually survival, meaning they do not want to get fired, they like their job, and they want to keep their job.

When you advance up the chain of command and you are speaking with middle management, your Call Plan will reflect that the attendees are likely responsible for figuring out how to implement an initiative to support their strategies, developing the budgets, and assigning resources to initiatives. They usually like to discuss cost instead of price, meaning their interests are more aligned to total cost of ownership and the return on investment. Their time frame is the present; they are concerned about the present, they have already learned from the past, and they are not too concerned with it. Their agenda is to tie something successful to their belt, so in speaking with middle managers, your words need to reflect cost, the present, and success.

When you reach the top of the food chain—the executives—you will know you are meeting with people responsible for establishing the corporate vision. The executives have established the strategic initiatives that middle management is responsible for implementing. Executives like to discuss value to the organization instead of cost and price. They also are keen to discuss responsibility and accountability. Their time frame or orientation is the future, meaning they want to know how the seller's solution will impact the future of the organization. Executives want to make a significant difference and leave a legacy.

What Information Do We Want to Convey?

Identifying this is critical to the seller's ability to communicate a message that is consistent and supports the strategy to win. People learn through repetition and relevance, so crafting a message that is consistent, repeatable, and relevant will help the seller seem organized and trustworthy. As well, it helps the seller bring all the materials necessary to support the information the team wants to convey.

High-Yield Questions

Defining in advance the information you must collect to move forward helps you formulate High-Yield Questions. The Call Plan should include both the information you need to advance and the questions you plan to use to yield that information. If this question does not result in the answer you were looking for, your team members can ask follow-up questions so that the sales team does not miss a golden opportunity to advance.

Competitive Traps

Competitive traps are not naturally occurring events. They need to be planned in advance for maximum effectiveness and minimal visibility to the buyer. Content is important, as is the person from the sales team who will deliver the trap to a specific buyer. Defining who gives and who receives the trap early on allows the relevant sales team member to listen for opportunities in the conversation to effectively communicate the competitive trap.

By defining the person responsible for delivering the competitive trap, you create a seemingly natural flow to the conversation. Without defining the person, one of two things will happen: (1) all sales team members aware of their objective to deliver the trap will start speaking on top of one another, or (2) an awkward pause will be inserted into the conversation as all sales team members aware of their objective to deliver the trap are silent for fear of talking on top of one another.

Handling Objections

If you were the buyer, what questions or objections might you have about your solution? When creating the Call Plan, determine what these questions might be, defining whether the question is a speed bump or a roadblock, as well as the solution you can deliver.

By identifying these objections, you can construct non-defensive responses and practice delivering them before you go on the call. You therefore appear prepared and look patient and confident in your response when the objection is raised. This is another true value of the Call Plan, especially if you have a sales team, as the team might not have considered the objections or the answers in advance of the call.

What Was Done Prior to the Meeting?

The last point to consider and communicate to the team is what activities were done prior to the call so everyone

RISK ... MITIGATE IT

is informed. For example, was the agenda circulated and approved by the attendees? Was the appointment confirmed? Were new people added to the call as a result of the confirmation? Were any documents sent ahead of time other than the agenda? Was the presentation you are using approved by the Coach?

This information sets everyone's expectations and addresses any objections that may arise.

CHAPTER 11

The Overview

Your Customer Game Plan

["Quality is never an accident; it is always the result of high intention, sincere effort, intelligent direction, and skillful execution; it represents the wise choice of many alternatives."
—William A. Foster, former U.S. Marine who received the Medal of Honor during World War II at the Battle of Okinawa]

One of our business partners used to say, "The best thing about a surprising loss is that it is not preceded by a period of worry and anxiety."

Good salespeople develop Customer Game Plans and execute those plans. Creating the plan requires analyzing the situation to determine strategy—specifically, the buyer's business, the people, and the competitive landscape. In many cases, this can cause anxiety. Analyzing the situation requires that you acknowledge your solution's weaknesses, which you might perceive to be a reflection of your ability. This anxiety causes too many salespeople to skip over this step—a big mistake!

Putting your head in the sand, i.e., proceeding without the analysis, is a good way to lose a deal. Understanding how to align your messages, activities, tools, and resources to support your strategy and to win the deal requires more effort than you may have planned. When working to land a new account or win a new opportunity, remember that what sounds straightforward and simple in theory is actually quite complex, requiring a Customer Game Plan that provides a framework for accomplishing the following:

o Aligning the internal team and organization with the game plan
o Interacting with the buyer's team
o Ensuring that the pace is consistent with the buyer's pace
o Dealing with outside consultants
o Addressing comments from industry analysts
o Recognizing that the competition has a viable solution in the eyes of the buyer
o Overcoming traps set by competitors
o Preparing the buyer to buy rather than displaying the bells and whistles of what you are selling

The Customer Game Plan, in short, is a compilation of every single tool and interaction we have discussed herein. The Call Plan defines one specific meeting; the Customer

Game Plan outlines each of the major steps that will occur in the selling process. It includes concepts that should now be very familiar to you:

1. The alignment of the buying and selling processes, which identifies the stages, milestones, and verifiable outcomes, which in turn drive the activities, tools, and skills you need to advance to the next level
2. Your analysis: the Collaboration Map, the Influence Map, and the Competitive Map that define your strategy
3. The Joint Evaluation Plan necessary to collaborate with the buyer on the buying process
4. The Call Plan that outlines the communication skills necessary to respond to competitive traps; formulate High-Yield Questions; communicate your advantages, values, and benefits; handle questions; and communicate success stories

In any given sales opportunity, the variables are vast and ever-changing. As you go through the process of discovery, you gain increasing insight into your buyer's organization, goals, objectives, and challenges by using tools such as the Collaboration Map, Influence Map, and Competitive Map. As you absorb this information, your responsibility as a salesperson is to decide how it will improve your position with the buyer by updating a Customer Game Plan that ensures you are doing what you know you should do.

But too often, sellers fail to implement the Customer Game Plan correctly. Though you likely know what you should be doing, sellers often fall short when it comes to execution. The silver bullet syndrome is often to blame. Sellers are always trying to speed things up: We need to close this deal this week. We know that the revenue is critical to our quarter-end numbers. The process is all about what *we* need on *our* time frames. In addition, with so many demands on our time, we are bombarded with e-mail at all hours of the night and day. We are always accessible by cell phone. We have internal systems that we have to keep updated. We are constantly fighting fires with customers. We barely have time to do it at all, much less do it right—a problem that almost guarantees we will have to do it again.

And so you want to skip right ahead to the close using some shortcut or another. While this might feel good, it creates discomfort for the buyer, who often misinterprets this as the seller ignoring the eye of the buyer.

The buyer needs time to process your offerings, both logically and emotionally, and if you do not understand the buyer's needs, or if you try to rush the buyer, you are not going to gain preference with that buyer. Consider what some buyers have reported about their sellers:

o "We spent time with the sales team sharing information about our project and our goals and objectives, and we never saw them use that information effectively."
o "They insisted that they spent time learning about our organization, but we still got a generic demo."
o "We asked for examples of how their solution would work in our business and for references specific to our industry. We didn't get either."

> **66** *We never have time to do it right,*
> *but we always have time to do it again.* **99**

Each of these negative reports is a result of a seller's trying to move things along too quickly. Creating a Customer Game Plan that is intentionally slow often means that the process moves along more quickly in the long run because the sales team not only knows what it should be doing, but it also executes. Consider the following benefits of stopping, assessing, and devising a plan.

1. The time spent on the front end developing the right plan makes the back end much shorter as you are executing on the plan, which makes the overall process shorter. This allows you to understand the buyer's business challenges, creates an opportunity to develop a relationship with the buyer, ensures that you are working a deal you can win before you spend resources, and provides visibility into the right strategy to win.
2. The size of the opportunity or engagement often gets larger without getting longer. Because you are providing a solution and not pushing a product, you are seen as a partner with the buyer as opposed to a sales representative. As a result, the buyer will bring more to your table.
3. You create a perception with the buyer as someone who has the buyer's business interests at heart. This generates not only the first sales, but also many sales thereafter, as buyers want to work with people who want to help them

instead of sell to them. By gaining an emotional competitive advantage, the seller receives information that the buyer might not otherwise disclose.

4. You learn whether you are losing before you give away all of your competitive information and trade secrets. When the buyer prefers a different seller, the buyer might inadvertently give away some of your competitive techniques. This information can hurt you on subsequent deals. Working a deal that you are sure to lose creates an unnecessary risk: you allow the competition to see how you operate, giving them a competitive advantage for many deals to come.

Communicating and Documenting the Plan

While salespeople may be strategic and exceptional planners, most do not communicate their plan well, nor do they document it. And this is the biggest problem with failing to distinguish between knowing and doing: sellers are good at their jobs (they know what to do), so they often do not take the time to document a plan, which they may consider sophomoric. As a result, they end up flying by the seat of their pants.

I'm good at my job, they think to themselves. *Selling is more of an art than a science. Writing a sales plan entails just a bunch of administrative bureaucracy that prevents me from making sales calls. Why make all this extra work when I could just get the job done?*

Hogwash. I can see why sales representatives who work alone might be reticent to document a plan no one else will read, but they are taking a risk by not documenting the process as a reminder of all the steps they need to take. Indeed, the challenge with failing to write the plan and document the competitive analysis is significant.

Memories Fade

As the saying goes, the faintest ink is more powerful than the strongest memory. As time slips by, sellers' memories tend to fade. They cannot remember why certain strategies were made, nor can they remember the buyers' objectives with precise accuracy. As a result, they may change their decisions without regard to the potential consequence of the change. They allow risks to present themselves. (Though no sales strategy is completely risk-free, we would much rather that a seller assess and choose risks strategically than open the doors for risks to present themselves willy-nilly.)

Sales representatives often get caught up in the day-to-day activities and do not remember the overarching strategy. As a result, the sales team might simply respond to buyer requests and random "strategies," believing the sale is advancing, when in fact, the sale has deviated from the planned strategy and the seller is responding only to what feels good or necessary. Without deliberate activities and specified results, sales reps miss the opportunity to close the deal sooner.

Perpetuate Hard-Won Institutional Knowledge

Without a written sales plan, teams may skip steps or forget to execute tactics that have worked in the past. I cannot tell you how many times InfoMentis has presented a workshop to a group of talented and experienced salespeople only to have them say things such as, "We used to do that, but we have dropped the ball on it lately."

No wonder their numbers have slipped!

Leverage Success

Unless they have documentation, sellers lose sight of activities they have performed for the buyer, which means they cannot leverage these activities to accelerate momentum in a deal. If you do not track or write down the activities you perform, you cannot articulate the value you have provided to the buyer, and you could be in a position of over-serving your buyer. This cycle—in which the buyer is asking, and you are doing without asking for anything in return—often turns around to bite the seller at the negotiation table.

In responding to requests without a specific strategy in mind, you face the danger of having trained the buyers to expect you to sacrifice on their behalf. When you refuse to acquiesce during negotiations, the buyer feels angry. If you spend the entire sales cycle teaching the buyers that you jump whenever they ask, the buyer feels taken advantage of and manipulated when you change the game during negotiations.

If the seller fails to provide tangible evidence, the buyer has no appreciation for the investment the seller has made on the buyer's behalf. Because the buyers are not tracking what you have done for them, they have no understanding of the effort, time, or resources you have provided. If the sales team also does not track the activities, it misses the opportunity to build a relationship based on fair trade. A buyer expects that the sales team is happy to exchange time and resources for something from the buyer in return. Exchanging value for value is, of course, the crux of fair trade.

A Unified Front

Without a written plan guiding their efforts, the sales team lacks understanding of analysis behind the strategy. When your team doesn't understand the strategy or why it was selected, their words, actions, and attitudes can derail the deal or create unnecessary risk. Skeptical buyers (and most are) are on the lookout for differences across sales teams. When a team is not executing on a consistent message, for example, the buyer responds by doubting the message. Though the buyer may never express this doubt, he or she will weigh it against the seller when selecting the ultimate solution.

Everyone's on the Same Page

The sales representative wastes endless hours bringing the team up to speed on the account. By creating a written plan, the seller can spend time discussing tactics to win and let the sales team read the background documentation. Spending time discussing how a team might win or why it might lose is productive only if the team understands the details of the opportunity. Having a documented plan saves countless hours later in the process.

Knowing what to do and actually doing the right things take tremendous discipline. Much like an airplane pilot who certainly knows how to fly, sellers must go through their checklist before every takeoff and every landing. As a seller, you need a pilot's checklist in every deal for the same reasons: so as to not forget to do what you know.

Alignment of the Buyer's and Seller's Processes

The first component requires you to create a written plan that considers each milestone of the *aligned* buying and selling processes. Remember each of the five stages:

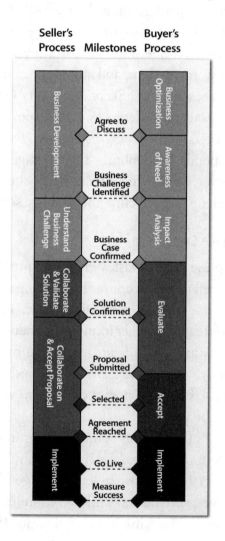

Seller's Process	Milestones	Buyer's Process
Business Development	Agree to Discuss	Business Optimization
	Business Challenge Identified	Awareness of Need
Understand Business Challenge	Business Case Confirmed	Impact Analysis
Collaborate & Validate Solution	Solution Confirmed	Evaluate
Collaborate on & Accept Proposal	Proposal Submitted	
	Selected	Accept
	Agreement Reached	
Implement	Go Live	Implement
	Measure Success	

For each of these five stages, be sure to identify milestones that measure progress. Remember that milestones represent a specific point in time within the process whereby the buyer and seller make sure they have achieved their goals to date. Make sure that each milestone you insert into the appropriate stage is verifiable, meaning that the seller can witness the buyer performing an action to verify that the buyer has arrived at that milestone.

Be sure to also include the specific goals you must achieve that earn you the right to move to the next phase.

Use Your Maps

In the second component, your Collaboration Map, Influence Map, and Competitive Map are all part of your Game Plan. Remember that these—like the Game Plan that encompasses them—are constantly changing as you move through the process and gain more context surrounding the buyer's needs and perception.

Joint Evaluation Plan

The third component of the Customer Game Plan is your Joint Evaluation Plan, which allows the seller to validate with the buyer the activities to be performed in order for the buyer to be confident with its decision to buy from you. The Joint Evaluation Plan from Chapter 7 allows you to gain the buyer's commitment to the evaluation project plan and validate your game plan to win.

The Call Plan

Finally, the Call Plan helps you measure whether the buyer is advancing by outlining the High-Yield Questions you will use for each stage of the process, as well as those you will use to help fill in your Collaboration Map, Influence Map, Competitive Map, and Joint Evaluation Plan. The Call Plan also helps you identify how you will communicate your advantages, respond to competitive traps, and communicate success stories. Be sure that a Call Plan is always prepared in advance.

Your Game Plan is not only constantly changing, but it also differs based on each unique client. Though the method is always the same, no one concrete set of activities can be used for each buyer. Instead, your Game Plan consists of the data you collect as you evaluate the eye of the buyers and consider their needs from their perspective.

THE WEDDING IS NOT THE END

CHAPTER 12

The Delivery

Let's fast-forward a bit and say that all of your hard work from the previous chapters has paid off and you have actually closed the business deal. OK, what now?

I'm sure you've heard of, even experienced, buyer's remorse. Buyers can easily become anxious once the decision has been made. Did they make the right choice? Did they cover all of the bases that they needed to? Will you deliver on your promises?

Buyers expect you to keep your promises, but at the same time, they are afraid that you won't. Keeping promises seems like a fair enough expectation, so why does it so often create angst with a new buyer?

There could be many reasons for the buyers' angst. Were they let down in the past? Did the sales team keep their promises during the sales cycle? Did the team thoroughly evaluate and validate the truth as you knew it at a specific point in time during the evaluation process? What did they miss in the evaluation that they should have asked? Buying something can lead to all kinds of potential for confusion and emotions.

There are two kinds of promises you make to your buyers—explicit and implicit. *Explicit promises* are easy to spot.

215

These might be your promise to get the solution implemented by a certain date or a price quote that you promise to stand by. Explicit promises are easy to understand, easy to document, easier to keep, and still easier to know when you haven't kept them.

Implicit promises are much more difficult because they may be vague. These are the ones you make but are not written into the agreements you sign. They are, however, just as real. The expectations that you will keep your verbal promises are every bit as important a part of your relationship with a buyer as your written promises. In fact, you either thrive or die by your implicit promises.

You seldom explicitly guarantee that your buyers will save a specific amount of money or improve customer service or employee satisfaction, but that's exactly the kind of promises you make by attaching your name and reputation to a solution. Those implicit promises go a long way in helping your buyers prefer and select you over the competition. Promises become expectations. You say or imply you will do something (or that a specific result will occur), and the buyer expects it to happen.

Since a buyer often interacts with multiple people during the selling process, keeping track of who promised what to whom and when can get challenging. This is one of the key reasons that the tools that provide collaboration among the team and with the buyer are so important.

Promise Makers and Promise Keepers

This problem is universal and can hurt you. Typically, the promise makers and the promise keepers are not the same individuals. The sales team may promise the solution by a certain date, but production and shipping may be unable to manufacture and ship it on or before the set date. Expectations are set in the buyer's mind, but development and product management have to make it actually happen. This is the difference between the promise makers and the promise keepers.

And this dilemma occurs often with assistants who let buyers know they will receive a call back from an executive within the next day. Promise made. Then in the crush of daily activities, the phone call is left unmade. Promise broken.

In today's world of hectic schedules, reorganizations, downsizings, and job sharing, keeping promises is increasingly difficult. However, difficult or not, you need to deliver on every promise you make, both explicit and implicit.

Success Includes Delivering on Your Promises

Your success in generating repeat buyers depends to no small degree on your ability to keep your promises to them. When you do, they feel you are reliable. They will trust you on an ongoing basis. Keeping your promises also helps perpetuate a sense of buyer-centeredness. Buyers like it when they see that your focus is primarily on making sure their business needs are met. It reflects credibly on their jobs and allows them to manage job risk, which ranks high in their needs. This kind of focus is easy to lose or, worse, to ignore.

Buyers are rightfully self-centered. They don't care about your year-end quotas, resource constraints, or corporate edicts to "do more with less." They care first and foremost about which vendors are best suited and able to deliver what was promised, when it was promised, and how much was promised. Every time you fail, you substantially dilute the trust that your buyer places in you. However, when you reliably deliver on your promises, you gain more trust. And when you repeatedly deliver on your promises, you elevate your customer relationship to even higher levels.

But—and this is a big principle—*trust is never established business-to-business; trust is established person-to-person.* A single point of trust is when an individual from the buying team has a trusted relationship with an individual from the selling team. Only people who deliver on their promises will be trusted by their customers.

Beyond a Single Point of Trust

A single point of trust is better than none. But if you have only a single point of trust in a relationship between the seller organization and the buyer, you face unnecessary risks. The risk works two ways: risk to the seller and risk to the buyer. What will you do if the trusted seller employee leaves? Who would the buyer trust going forward? Conversely, what happens if your buyer reorganizes and the person with whom your salesperson has established a relationship is no longer in a position to do business with you? Up to a point, you can rely on the fact that you've done business with that buyer before, but you have to start from square one on establishing a sense of trust and comfort. This takes time, money, energy, and effort. There's a better way.

Use a team approach. Coordinate the team to support a single point of relationship accountability, allowing multiple points of trust. At InfoMentis, every one of our clients has a single point of accountability—a "CEO" for the account—yet many trusted relationships. It's important that others in your organization establish and maintain relationships within the buyer organization as well. This helps both sides of the relationship deal with inevitable change over time.

Creating Buyer-Centric Reliability

When we talk of a buyer-centric culture, we're talking about a paradigm shift, not just about a sales process. Our interest is in the culture.

Buyer-Centric Is Not Just a Slogan

When Copernicus proclaimed that the earth revolves around the sun, instead of the sun around the earth, this marked a major paradigm shift in humankind's thinking. His discovery changed our entire understanding of the way the universe works. It helped us go on to make more amazing discoveries.

When we say buyer-centric we mean to change the way you look at your business universe. It isn't a slogan. It goes beyond just thinking about the buyer. It's a complete shift to viewing the world from the buyer's point of view. Without this shift of perspective, it's like going back to the pre-Copernican universe—at least in terms of the business world.

The Buyer-Centric Team

If you want to create a customer-centric culture of reliability, then every person in your organization who touches the customer must adopt the customer-centric attitude. A customer-centric sales team is a wonderful thing, but if your service and support teams are not customer-centric, then the overall level of customer trust can drop dramatically.

Audit What You Have Delivered

We have a rule at InfoMentis: nothing goes out the door without another set of eyes reviewing it. Proposals, training materials, win/loss analyses, maintenance retention benchmarks—everything! Does that mean we are flawless? Nope, but we are a lot better off than if we didn't follow this rule.

You will be amazed how much you can see when you are not as close to the deliverable as the person who created it. Maybe an extra set of eyes will notice a simple thing, such as an extra period at the end of a sentence. It doesn't matter if the mistake is major or not. Quality comes from a review process, and the better the quality, the better that perception by the recipient. But an internal review process is not enough; it captures only the errors we catch. It cannot measure how the buyer perceives the deliverable.

So we audit our customers. We send Web-based surveys to random members of our customer base, and from their feedback, we constantly track the job we are doing. We ask not only about the services we provide but also about our reliability, quality, and customer-centeredness. If we find a problem, we would much rather know about it early so we can correct it. Earlier is better than later, and knowing is better than not knowing. You know the saying: bad news early is good news.

When we conduct a training session, we not only track the "smile sheets" (workshop evaluations) and help our customers deploy their new programs, but we also regularly check back with the participants to measure results and make sure they are continuing to monitor the programs we provide. This is because we promise more than simply training: we promise behavior change. If we do not help our customers implement and then audit what we have delivered, we will never know if the buyers got the value we promised them. Consider the outcomes of delivering what you promise.

When one of our largest customers, a prominent Fortune 500 company, came to us to buy something that we didn't have, we wondered why they came to us in the first place. They knew we did not have exactly what they were looking for. We eventually discovered that they wanted us to develop the program they needed from scratch. From previous dealings, they trusted us and knew we were reliable. Their trust in our ability to create realistic promises gave us an edge that was hard to come by any other way. They paid us to develop a program customized to them, even though it was available as off-the-shelf training from other providers.

That kind of confidence doesn't come from the sellers taking a shortcut, or indulging in immediate gratification, or immersing themselves in a silver bullet culture. It requires the customer's trust across our organization—the sales team, the development team, the delivery team, and all of the rest of it. For us, it means that everyone has to be on board with the buyer-centered culture we insist upon.

As more people within your organization take personal responsibility for keeping their promises, it becomes important that everyone in your organization shares and keeps promises. Then your customer's confidence in you, your team, and your company will grow.

A Confidence Test

We use this list to help vendors evaluate the confidence their buyers have in them. It helps to separate the emotional feeling that a seller has secured a buyer's confidence from the objective evidence on whether this is really true. Take a look at this list and ask yourself if your buyers are displaying these behaviors:

- ○ They actively seek your advice.
- ○ They accept and act on your recommendations; they don't make you compete for every opportunity.
- ○ They involve you in more strategic, complex issues in their business.
- ○ They share information about their business (pipeline, revenue, challenges, etc.).
- ○ They introduce or refer you to other sources of business or partnerships.
- ○ They allow more mistakes and grant you the benefit of the doubt.
- ○ They display increased loyalty.
- ○ They raise issues sooner rather than later.

The Principle
❝ *If you want repeat buyers, deliver what you promise.* **❞**

EPILOGUE

THE CHAIR AND THE ASS, PART TWO

"Trust me, this is not where I was planning on spending New Year's Eve," Chelsea tells her boss. She has been sitting outside the buyer's office for three days, hoping to get his signature and close the deal.

Meanwhile, on the other side of the wall sits Larry. Upon joining the Outstanding Options team, he quickly moved up through the ranks. By always considering the eye of the buyer and training his colleagues to do the same, he had not only won Hargrove's continued business, but he also improved Outstanding Options' sales numbers significantly during his first year. Eventually, he was promoted to CIO of the company.

And now he was responsible for deciding whether to do business with Chelsea's company.

Damned salespeople! Larry thought as he contemplated Chelsea's strategy. *I cannot believe that woman is still sitting out there. We have told her over and over that this project is important to us, and we have told her that we prefer her solution. She was nothing but accommodating while she was making the sale, but now she wants me to do this on her timeline!*

Larry considered simply packing his bags. He could easily walk away and enjoy his New Year's Eve, making her miss her year-end sales goal.

That'll teach her, he thought.

And then he reconsidered. After all, he had been in her shoes before. *I'm just being cranky,* he thought to himself, taking a deep breath. Finally, he called her in.

"Chelsea," he tells her, "I'm sorry to keep you waiting. I know what it's like to be sitting on the other side of that wall. I started as a sales rep for Outstanding Options, so I can easily relate to your frustration.

"But the problem is this: *I* shouldn't be the one relating to *you.* You should be considering my perception. Instead, you are rushing me through this process, browbeating me into signing this contract so you can meet your sales goals. I'm *your* client. The only timeline you should be considering is mine."

Chelsea is aghast. She wonders, *What is my boss going to do if I lose this deal?*

Larry continues, "I know what you are thinking. You are thinking you might lose this deal and that your boss will be furious if you don't meet your year-end quota."

He had hit the nail on the head.

"You see, when you don't take a moment to sit back and consider what I call 'the eye of the buyer,' you appear very self-serving. You don't seem to want to help me find a solution that meets my needs."

Larry continues. When all is said and done, he has spent an hour telling Chelsea about the silver bullet, showing her how Outstanding Options uses

Collaboration Maps, Influence Maps, Joint Evaluation Plans, Call Plans, Competitive Maps, High-Yield Questions, and Game Plans to make sure they are always considering the eye of the buyer.

By the time he signs the contract, Chelsea is breathing a sigh of relief. Sure, she is glad she met her quota, but she is more excited to finally have a strategy that stops the endless pursuit of the silver bullet.

INDEX

ABOUT INFOMENTIS

InfoMentis improves the revenue performance of client organizations by challenging the standard training model with innovative solutions. InfoMentis leverages training, consulting, and enabling technologies such as Dealmaker to create an environment that drives adoption.

InfoMentis's expertise is centered around how buyers buy. We specialize in helping clients create repeat buyers and predictable revenue streams by aligning their organization's processes, skills, and disciplines to make training work. InfoMentis takes complex problems and distills them into a repeatable process in order to achieve a client's desired business results.

InfoMentis is headquartered in Alpharetta, Georgia. For more information about InfoMentis, please visit:

www.infomentis.com

or e-mail us at info@infomentis.com.